MEMORIES OF DURHAM

The publishers would like to thank the following companies for their

support in the production of this book

Main Sponsor

Esh Group

Bramwell Jewellers

Hillside Plastics Ltd

Land Registry

L G Philips Displays

Northumbian Water Limited

PSI Global

Three Rivers Housing Group

Veriplast International

Ward Bros. Plant Hire Ltd

J W Wood

First published in Great Britain by True North Books Limited
England HX3 6AE
01422 344344

ISBN 1 903204 81 X

Text, design and origination by True North Books Limited
Printed and bound by The Amadeus Press Limited

Introduction from the Esh Group

We are delighted to help bring Durham Memories to you. The companies that have come together to form the Esh Group have so many links throughout the whole of County Durham - it is very fitting that we should be closely involved with a lasting record such as this.

The landscape of County Durham today largely reflects its mining and industrial past. Today's businesses are mostly of a new breed: smaller, more flexible and spread across every sector. We in the Esh Group typify this new breed, but we remain very conscious of our roots. Coal mining was the lifeblood of the villages in which our families were raised. We have succeeded by taking advantage of the many changes in fortune that have impacted upon the Region. We are deeply grateful to everyone who has worked in all the companies of this group over the last thirty two years and we are very proud of their achievements.

We believe that we have had a major part to play in building the County Durham of today. We have worked to restore and maintain the fabric of the County whilst also having a hand in many of the more recent additions to the built environment. We look forward to building the County Durham of the future in the years ahead.

This publication is a wonderful testament to the work of businesses such as ours. It also provides access to a superb archive of material. It is very fitting that we should play a key role in bringing this nostalgic publication to you. Our focus is now on the future and we face it with eager anticipation and confidence. We believe that our County of Durham is well placed to grow and prosper in the years ahead.

Thank you for all your support in the past. We hope that you and your businesses will also prosper in the future and that we do this together.

ESH GROUP

Contents

Introduction

Durham is a proud city with a distinguished heritage dating back well over 1,000 years. Today it boasts a handsome castle, distinguished cathedral, prestigious university and a city centre that retains much of its historic atmosphere. Yet, alongside those aesthetic delights, there beats a traditional working class heart that is illustrated in Durham's determination to retain its links with the days when coal was king. This juxtaposition, but still integration, of lofty culture and northern grit helps make our city almost unique in Britain, which is why we love it so. In 'Memories of Durham' readers will get a true flavour of its place in our hearts as we recall the middle years of the last century when the pace of life was different, as were many of our values.

Our world is changing so quickly that there seldom seems time to stop for a moment and check on the period through which we have lived. We are constantly looking forward to what lies ahead without considering that we have left behind. If we are not careful the lessons and the achievements of the past will become lost forever, consigned to some distant, dusty recess of our brains that can no longer be accessed. 'Memories of Durham' is a publication that will help unlock the key to the historically recent times through which our parents and we lived. Already many of us have forgotten or never fully experienced life as it was before the onset of relief roads and motorway links. There really was an age, not too long ago, when the car did not reign supreme and when children played with homemade toys without the need of computer chips with everything. We had food that tasted of something other than plastic, people went shopping in the market for fresh fruit instead of designer jeans from the mall and families sat round tables together to eat their evening meals. They listened to the radio, grouped in front of a crackling set that brought 'Dick Barton', 'ITMA' and Henry Hall's orchestra into the front room. Out on the streets rag and bone men called out for business, offering to exchange unwanted household scrap for pegs to be used on the washing line and donkey stones to enhance the appearance of the doorstep.

Within the pages of this book the reader will be able to

return to those days when our monarchs were revered and our newsreels were full of British achievement. At the same time you will be able to see Durham and its people once more; when we drank in pubs rather than theme bars and youths spoke with one another instead of punching text keys on their mobile phones. 'Memories of Durham' contains many stunning and evocative photographs, accompanied by informative and wry text that is intended to provoke discussion as much as it is written to illuminate the scene.

This is not a dry, dusty definitive history and, although the book concentrates on the half century that starts just after the first world war, to understand that era better we must briefly consider the developments over the previous years that shaped the 20th century. Durham, meaning hill on an island, was founded by a group of monks who settled here, having moved from Lindisfarne where they had guarded the body of St Cuthbert for some 300 years since his death in 687. A much revered saint, his resting place had become a place of pilgrimage, but was threatened by a series of Viking raids in the 10th century. The arrival of the monks in Durham, and with them St Cuthbert's remains, soon gave rise to it becoming a focal point for religious interest. As Durham's core is located on a peninsula in a bend of the River Wear, it was a natural defensive site and was chosen by William the Conqueror as a fortress and bulwark against the Scots to the north. It soon became a seat of the feudal prince-bishops entrusted with the defence of the northern region of the nation. The castle, built in 1072 to protect the narrow neck of the peninsula on its northern side, was until 1836 one of the palaces of the bishopric. Work on the magnificent cathedral began in 1093 and took 40 years to complete, but its presence today as a centre of interest for tourists who marvel at its majesty is a fine testament to the skill and eye for beauty possessed by our medieval forefathers.

New areas outside the peninsula were established in the 12th century and included Elvet, the borough of St Giles and Bishops Borough. Although flour milling and wool fulling were significant commercial activities at this time, there was mention made of coal mining as early as 1183 with early drift mines providing the fuel for heating iron used in the making of ploughs. It was the Durham monks who were the first to mine coal from primitive pits and by 1350 they worked deposits at

Lumley, Rainton and Ferryhill. However, this industry was more significant in the outlying districts and a coal mining enterprise in Elvet in the 19th century proved to be short-lived. Durham's greater claim to fame lay through its growth as an educational and religious centre. By the early 15th century, the Almoners School, next to the priory, and a choir school had been established, quickly followed by grammar and music schools on Palace Green.

By the middle of the 18th century Durham had grown to a population of over 4,000, but the coming of the industrial revolution that changed the face and size of so many other north country towns largely passed us by in our native city. There were woollen factories, some iron works, carpet making, organ building, breweries, mustard making and paper mills that developed in the 19th century, helping the population to grow to some 14,000, but that degree of increase did not continue in later Victorian times. Even by the end of Victoria's reign there were just 16,000 inhabitants on record and there are still less than double that figure living here today. Our famous seat of learning was founded in 1832 as Britain's third university and the Bishop gave the castle for use as a college five years later. But more down to earth, or even underground, interests were to make their mark in the latter years of the 1800s and the early ones of the following century. The first miners' gala was held in 1871 and, by 1919, Britain saw its first Labour controlled county council when it assembled at Shire Hall.

It is from just after this time that 'Memories of Durham' can take over and whisk the reader off on a journey through times that can be regarded as modern history and those for which many of us have a keen interest as it is around the corner from some of our own recollections and just within reach for others. Get in the mood for those days when computers were unknown and hardware was screws, nuts and bolts, and chips came with salt and vinegar. Let the waves of nostalgia wash all over you as you suck on a Spangle, light up a pipe full of thick twist or straighten the seam in your stocking. It is time to turn the first page and embark on a journey when you could call someone 'love' or 'hen' and not be accused of being sexist, mainly because the word had not been invented. There was an age when men wore the trousers and women the earrings, so let us now go there.

Street Scenes

Below: This is the original statue of Neptune, with its famous pant or dinking fountain, seen a year or so before its removal to Wharton Park in 1923. Since 1729 it had stood at the wellhead, the only source of public water supply in Durham until 1849. The pant was supplied by water piped from nearby Crook Hall. A circular block now marks Neptune's original siting and was placed there to commemorate the formal opening of the restorative paving of Market Place and the medieval city centre streets in a ceremony conducted by Mayor James Mackintosh on 21 July 1976. As the Roman god of the sea, Neptune would appear to be a strange choice of statue for an inland city. However, in the early 18th century there were plans afoot to turn Durham into a port by widening the River Wear and linking the city to the Tyne via a canal. In 1759 there was also another scheme considered for making the Wear navigable to Sunderland, but as ships were rapidly increasing in size, this became a non-starter. Neptune, who returned to Market Place in 1991, is a reminder of those rather optimistic proposals. Market Tavern is to the left of the pant and is the place where the Miners' Union was formed in 1871. Market Place itself once housed a large covered market in front of St Nicholas' Church. From 1780 it was a busy, buzzing place that brought in farmers and traders from out of town and was a popular place for street entertainers to earn a living performing for the shoppers coming to market.

Above: Old Elvet in the early 1920s, photographed with the Royal County Hotel, now a part of the Marriott chain, on the left and Rutherford's newsagent and bookseller on the opposite corner, had a water fountain or pant in the centre of its cobbled roadway. The long, straight street leads from the bridge to the right hand bend in the distance that curves away towards the prison that dates from 1810. Old Elvet was once the site of Durham's horse fair and is where remains of an Iron Age fort and a Roman villa have been unearthed, confirming this part of the city's links with antiquity. This street contains many statuesque buildings that hail from the Georgian period and give an imposing atmosphere to the roadway that they front. However, as grand as they were, they lacked running water and residents had to rely on wells and springs, supplemented by the pant that was erected in 1863. It was removed before the start of the last war and, by then, all the homes had been connected to the mains for some time. The Waterloo Hotel, to the left of the fountain, was demolished in 1960 as part of the road widening scheme. The photographer was standing with his back to Elvet Bridge, the landmark that has been in daily use since it was built by Hugh Puiset or Pudsey, Bishop of Durham (1153-95), in around 1160. It has been repaired and altered on many occasions since then.

Below: Framwellgate was once part of the old coaching route to the north. The improved North Road replaced it as the main road in the 1830s. This general view of Framwellgate in around 1930 shows much of the housing that was demolished when the Sherburn Road estate was built. It looks quite picturesque to anyone hankering back to the days when our city more resembled a quiet, medieval spot, rather than a bustling, modern city. In truth, many of the houses were damp and unhealthy places in which to raise a family. We only have to look in churchyards to realise the problems presented by poor living conditions, lack of hygiene and limited medical care to our forefathers in the late 19th and early 20th centuries. Headstones, marked with the names of so many young children and those of adults who died before their time, bring a tear to the most hardened of eyes. Achieving their allotted three score and ten years was out of reach for ordinary folk. The average life expectancy in late Victorian times was not much more than 45. By the 1930s things had improved, thanks to advances in medicine, particularly with regard to nursing techniques. The development of penicillin, discovered by Alexander Fleming in 1928, would help even more. In the meantime, councils recognised the need for decent housing and embarked on programmes of providing clean, affordable accommodation.

Right: Next door but one to Doggart's store, William Smith and Company ran a family draper's shop on Market Place in the 1930s. This was a difficult decade in Durham and across the country in general. Britain just did not seem able to recover from the economic disaster that was one of the legacies of the Great War. Prime Minister Lloyd George had promised the nation that he would see to it that the government built 'a land fit for heroes', but it appeared to everyone else that it was a long time coming. Throughout the 1920s there was unrest and ill feeling as the lot of the working classes seemed worse rather than better. Miners, in particular, felt the pinch and, when the general level of wages was cut, adopted the slogan 'Not a penny off the pay, not a minute on the day'. There was little sign of improved living conditions and ordinary people felt betrayed. Things came to a head with a general strike in 1926 and, combined with the effect of the 1929 stock market crash in America, Britain entered the 1930s reeling from the aftershock. By the mid 1930s there were 3 million out of work. Durham made some belated attempts to provide a better life for its inhabitants and, not before time, introduced a programme of slum clearance in Millburngate, Framwellgate and Old Elvet. Many residents from there were rehoused on the new estate on Sherburn Road. Shopkeepers, such as those around Market Place, felt the pinch with money being short and families unable to spend freely in these establishments.

Above: The lady shopper may have been sucking on an acid drop or perhaps the photographer caught her unawares outside the grocer's in 1937. The shop assistant was putting the finishing touches to an array of goods designed to tempt even the most ardent bargain-seeking housewife. Lovely fresh produce, tasting of the real thing and not like the mundane muck we buy in cellophane packets from modern supermarkets, was all there to tickle the taste buds. Children of today do not understand that we once bought sausages from the butcher, flowers from the florist, tea from the grocer, cigarettes from the tobacconist and cabbage from the greengrocer. They think that you get them on aisle six, eight and nine. Their little brains would also be addled if trying to cope with the mysteries of shillings and pence and goodness only knows what they would have made of half a stone of spuds. Buying our food today has become simpler and quicker, but those with a long memory would deny that it is any better. Gone is the special knowledge that a particular shopkeeper could draw upon to advise a customer. How can anyone have confidence in a spotty youth on the meat counter telling us which is the most economical cut of beef for a tasty stew when he has been stacking shelves with ready to wear shirts in the clothing department just half an hour earlier?

Right: Huge crowds filled Market Place on 23 January 1936 when Mayor, Councillor Gray, stood outside the Town Hall/Guildhall to address the multitude. Children from local schools were also in the throng that sang the national anthem with great gusto. The proclamation that was read out announced that we had a new king, Edward VIII. This ceremony is always one that keeps a fine balance between sadness and joy as it marks the death of one monarch as it recognises the succession of the next. George V passed away three days earlier, with the formal proclamation being read in London on the following day. Copies were subsequently brought to town halls all over Britain for relaying to the general public over the next few days. The old king had become a popular figure with his subjects, particularly when he did away with the Saxe-Coburg-Gotha family name in 1917, during World War I, replacing it with the House of Windsor. He was a plain speaker, especially when referring to foreigners and the resort of Bognor where he convalesced in 1929, following serious illness. His son was also well liked, though some did comment on his raffish lifestyle. Little were the people in Market Place to know that, as they shouted 'God save the king', they would be shocked and scandalised when news of his affair with Wallis Simpson became public knowledge.

Above: Love is blind and this could not be more true for Mr JW Vest and Miss Annie Morrison on 10 August 1939. Both of them were visually impaired, as we say nowadays, but their disability had not affected the path of real love and affection. They had just left the Registry Office on Claypath after tying the knot and, by the look on their faces, were chuffed to death to have done so. The happy couple were being anxiously watched by a group of wedding guests as they passed the offices of the Grange Coal and Durham Brick and Tile companies. The onlookers need not have worried because there seemed to be something optimistically fateful about another firm's name on the plate on the door pillar. That belonged to Ferens and Love, a sure omen of good fortune it seemed. Mr Vest came from Hatfield View, New Elvet and his blushing bride was a native of Burnhope. They probably did not have the advantage of some of the modern aids more freely available today, as guide dogs were only introduced on a limited scale in the late 1920s, following trials in Germany to assist blinded soldiers from the first world war. Even Braille, although in use for 100 years, was not standardised in the English speaking world until 1932. None of that really mattered to the new Mr and Mrs Vest as they only had eyes for each other.

Below: J Tuke and Son ran this music shop at 71 North Road in October 1938. Many families, and not just the middle classes, owned a piano that stood proudly in the corner of the best room. Many was the singsong families had in those days as they made their own entertainment. Neighbours and relatives often got together for their own version of the music hall or variety concert. Children were encouraged to do their party pieces. Little Ronnie sang 'When father papered the parlour' and young Doris performed a tap dance as dad tickled the ivories with 'Alexander's Ragtime Band' as an accompaniment. There was always someone who could play the spoons and grandad was a wow on the old concertina. Records were played on old wind-up gramophones, but there was no such thing as a top ten of pop record sales, because such a chart was not instituted until 1952. As well as musical instruments, Tuke sold sheet music with arrangements for popular songs of the day and it was the volume of this business that provided people with information as to which were the current favourite ditties. 'A nice cup of tea', 'September in the rain' and 'The folks who live on the hill' were all good antidotes for the grim news coming to us across the radio airwaves and on the front pages of our newspapers. Hitler's army had just marched into Czechoslovakia.

Above: The bus station, as it looked in the 1940s, had a distinctive ironwork frontage that was supplied and erected by the Lion Foundry Company in 1929. Designed by Chester-le-Street's Albert Funnel, the station was built in the grounds of a house built in 1842 for Mr Robson, the owner of a corn mill. His house became the bus station offices and the stream that served Robson's mill was culverted. Part of the arcading was taken down in the 1970s and stored at Beamish. Over half a century ago, this was the main focal point for people getting into and out of the city. Private car ownership was for the middle classes and the rest of us could neither afford the cost of buying a car nor even aspire ever to doing so. That would have to wait until the late 1950s when prices dropped and wages rose in a more stable economy. Before then we went to work, to school or off for a night out on that reliable form of public transport. Each bus had a conductor who detested any passenger with a ten shilling note, muttering under his breath about people who had more money than sense. He also had the wonderful knack of being able to ring the bell, telling the driver to set off, at the very moment that a potential passenger, late for an appointment, sprinted to get on board, failing by a matter of inches.

Below: This 1950s' photograph shows the rear of the bus station with its extended bays and features a variety of single and double decker buses. As the decade went on our reliance on the bus as our favoured mode of transport began to wane with the increase in the number of cars on the road. Family motoring was with us and Morris Minors, Ford Populars and BMC Minis were filled with those who used to depend on public transport to get around. That cultural change was not without its problems, particularly as Durham's streets were more medieval than modern. The sheer volume of traffic, even in those days, was a major headache. However, it took until 1963 for an inquiry to be mounted into the need for reducing traffic, improving access and overhauling shopping centres in the historic city. Although the first section of the new motorway, the A1(M), was commenced further south in 1965, this only had a limited effect on the city. Traffic congestion there was eased somewhat when Millburngate Road Bridge opened in 1967, along with the A690 link to Sunderland. Road widening near Elvet Bridge and the building of a new road bridge here in the 1970s also helped, but the narrow nature of the inner city streets meant that access to the centre was difficult. Fortunately, heritage won out over practicality and we were spared becoming a clone town, the fate of so many other British centres that were built to almost identical plans in the 1970s. Durham kept its identity and cars were largely restricted to the city outskirts.

A rather bemused bobby surveyed the scene on Saddler Street at its junction with Elvet Bridge, near the Magdalen Steps, in March 1951. Saddler Street was the entertainment centre of Durham in the 18th and 19th centuries, being home to a variety of drinking houses, theatres and a cockpit. However, the constable regarded the hay lorry on its side and the load scattered across the carriageway as a drama production that he could have well done without. Small knots of amused spectators, gathered outside the shops belonging to FW Hunter and T Henderson or on the opposite pavement, making what they thought were witty comments. One onlooker suggested that the officer should sing 'Hey, good looking', while another recommended a revised version of 'Strawberry blonde', emphasising the first syllable. Apparently, the lorry driver had got his bearings wrong by trying to turn back on himself by going right onto Elvet Bridge, when he should have been heading along Saddler Street to Market Place where he could swing round the traffic control box and then proceed back down and across the bridge without the need for such a difficult and, in fact illegal, manoeuvre. Whatever the cause, the policeman knew the effect. He was going to be on point duty for the next couple of hours as congestion built up with motorists getting hot under the collar waiting for the obstruction to be cleared away. The only appropriate song for him now was the one about the policeman's lot not being a happy one.

Above: It must have been a grim summer in June 1951 because these marchers are well wrapped up, considering the time of year. When looking at photographs from over half a century ago it is interesting to take in the fashion styles favoured by young and old, men and women. The young girl under the second banner is a real bobby-soxer, with her little white ankle socks. Can you imagine any child wearing them today? In the centre, the woman with the banner from the Durham City Pelaw Ward wore her dress with the hemline at a mid calf length. This was typical postwar fashion as women turned away from the shorter austerity clothing necessitated by the shortage of dress material as rationing took its toll on the way a girl looked. Although clothing coupons were still needed, supplies were more plentiful. This woman shows how our vital statistics have changed over the last 50 or more years. She had a trim, well defined figure with a waspish waist that measured about 26 inches, on average. Modern woman is, to put it politely, more rounded and her stomach has expanded by about seven inches. The men in the picture were all conformists, wearing the regulation suits, shirts, ties and homburgs. Councillor Wilf Edge stood in front of the Pelaw banner, with those from Easington Lane and Hetton behind, as the Women's Labour Gala stopped outside the Royal County Hotel.

Below: The women's sections of the Witton Park and Escomb Labour Party were coming past the County Hotel on Old Elvet in the summer of 1953. The hotel balcony provided a platform from where party and mineworker leaders would acknowledge the parade each gala day. Inside is the black staircase that dates from 1660, said to have been brought from Loch Leven Castle where Mary, Queen of Scots, signed her abdication papers in 1567. The marching women were proud of their socialist beliefs and were keen supporters of the political party that had swept Clement Attlee to power in 1945. However, by the time of this procession, Churchill was back in charge and these women would see a total of four Tory Prime Ministers in office before one of their own, Harold Wilson, regained the keys of 10 Downing Street. The procession was making its way towards Elvet Bridge along one of Durham's widest and most impressive streets, with its 18th century buildings and copper-domed Victorian Shire Hall. Elvet takes its name from the old English 'aelfet-ee', meaning swan island. It was in this vicinity that the city of Durham's only coalmines were once situated. Eight were in operation in the 19th century, though there were many more in the adjacent countryside.

Above: Camera, action! The newsreel operator made sure that he got a good view in front of the Evening Chronicle offices in Market Place over the heads of those who had come along to see Field Marshal Montgomery on 14 January 1953. The children, well swathed in balaclavas, warm coats and school caps, looked somewhat nonplussed by the occasion. They were told that an important person was visiting, but they had no real knowledge of what a field marshal was. The boys wondered if it was something to do with Roy Rogers or Hopalong Cassidy as the only marshals they knew of rode horses, fired sixshooters and wore silver stars on their chests. They were in for a disappointment, because no one was going to ride Trigger or Topper into the square. Instead, a middle-aged man in a beret was the centre of attraction. The children's parents knew all about him, because Montgomery was one of the leading figures of the second world war. After his exploits against the Desert Fox, General Rommel, in the North African campaign, he was afforded the honour of being referred to by the diminutive 'Monty'. Just as Churchill became 'Winnie', so our army hero was given the same type of endearing nickname. Both men could be grumpy, but they shared the common touch that won the hearts of the nation.

Right: Rag week is that peculiarly British occasion when gifted students are allowed to act like idiots and create modest mayhem in a charitable cause. Successive older generations have commented that such behaviour is typical of their normal life, anyway, but the grey haired brigade has probably forgotten what it got up to in its youth. Dignitaries were kidnapped and ransomed, collection boxes rattled under shoppers' noses and joke books, containing a mix of the puerile and the risqué, were sold to raise funds for hospitals, children, animal rescue and other laudable causes. The fancy dress parade along Silver Street on 1 February 1957, using lories and carts donated by business for transformation into floats, attracted locals onto the pavement who watched with some amusement at the antics of the brainy sections of our society. The young people attired in ridiculous garb would go on to become teachers, lawyers, doctors, historians, politicians and scientists where they would be expected to dress formally and behave in a cultured manner. They could be forgiven their eccentricities on this occasion, though the wary housewife made sure that she kept a careful eye on the students holding the water pistol and the bag of flour. The parade passed 39 Silver Street that stood, until its demolition in 1964, as the former home of Sir John Duck (1632-91), a former Mayor of Durham. Clinton's card shop and Phones4U now use the site.

Above: FW Woolworth has been a fixture on the high streets of nearly every English town and city since the interwar years. The five and ten cent store, established in America in the 19th century, has become synonymous with cheap and cheerful goods and is now seen as being as British as fish and chips. We even give it the affectionate term of 'Woolie's', just as we would to an old friend. The women's gala procession, showing the Labour Party section from Tantobie and Tanfield Lee, paraded down Silver Street, that medieval and narrow thoroughfare that is still one of the busiest shopping areas in the city. It is thought to take its name from the mint where Durham coinage was produced in the times of the Prince Bishops. Lower down, farriers used to operate in the vicinity of Framwellgate Bridge and this part of Silver Street was originally known as Smithgate. The line of women marching in July 1954 is a reminder of the powerful role they held in the life of the mining community. They held the family together and were fiercely supportive of their menfolk, especially in times of strife. Who can forget the images of such determined wives and mothers in the bitter wrangles with the government during the strikes in the 1980s, scenes repeated from similarly acrimonious conflicts in earlier years?

Below: Neptune has been absent from Market Place for most of our lives as the old chap was only returned in 1991, having spent 68 years in the wilderness at Wharton Park. In this picture from the late 1950s, the Marquess of Londonderry had been used to a lonely vigil for some 35 years. The view, looking towards Silver Street, has changed little in the intervening years, though the motorcars in the centre would now be unwelcome guests. The names on the shops have altered to Chapman, Thomas Cook, WH Smith, Music Zone and Lloyds TSB, but the buildings have stayed the same. How lucky we are when compared with the monstrosities that 1970s' architects brought to market squares and places in other towns, gutting the heritage and replacing it with uniform rectangles of glass, steel and concrete. The statue of Charles William Vane Tempest Stewart, to give the Marquess his full list of names, is a fine example of electroplating. It was unveiled on 2 December 1861 as a tribute to the dashing soldier and Lord Lieutenant of Durham who became a local colliery owner and found further fame as the builder of Seaham harbour. It was designed by Monti, an Italian sculptor, and erected on the site of the old market house. The statue was given a facelift in 1952.

Below: The Durham County Advertiser display was mounted outside St Nicholas Church on 20 August 1959 during a seven week long newspaper strike. At least people moving across Market Place from the direction of Timothy White's could get a cup of coffee in the church, even if they did not have a paper to read as they took a short break from their shopping expeditions. Snippets of news on the boards only whetted the appetite for in-depth analysis of what was happening around the city or across the world. Most of us still did not own televisions, so newspapers were a major source of information that we relied on. But things would soon change. Even some reactionary politicians started to realise the power of the new media. Prime Minister Harold Macmillan was televised in conversation with President Eisenhower in a broadcast relayed from 10 Downing Street. Nicknamed the 'Ike and Mac' show, it heralded the age of 'image' that modern politicians have now taken to extremes with their toothy smiles and clever soundbites. Macmillan may have been a member of the old guard, but he was a canny wheeler dealer. When feedback from his TV appearance suggested that viewers were impressed with the way he controlled the influential American president he called a snap election. The Tories were returned with a majority of 100. In an understatement, 'Supermac' said, 'I think it went rather well'.

Right: This sextet of little imps probably did not know Guy Fawkes from Guy Burgess, but that mattered little as they pursued the early autumn tradition of collecting a penny for the guy. Alan Dickson, Tony Greaves, Eddie Jenkins, Alan Greaves, Peter Hughes and Vic Richardson could charm anyone with their winning smiles. On 3 November 1955 they practised the art of getting a neighbour to open her purse strings on Eddie's mum in Annand Road, Gilesgate. Their guy, made from old, cast off clothing and stuffed with a mixture of rags and newspaper, did not truly resemble the arch plotter who tried to blow up Parliament in 1605, but no one really cared. It was more important that the boys were continuing a tradition that was part and parcel of British life, along with new clothes for Whit walks, the conker season and bob-a-job week. It is so sad that pushing a vaguely human shape from door to door on the days leading up to bonfire night has largely disappeared from our culture. Parents are so fearful that their offspring will become victims of some appalling assault that they have outlawed them from such a harmless pastime. Is this a true reflection on the malaise of modern society or is it a case of parental paranoia? Whatever the answer, we know that the children of today have to miss out on such harmless fun enjoyed by their parents and grandparents.

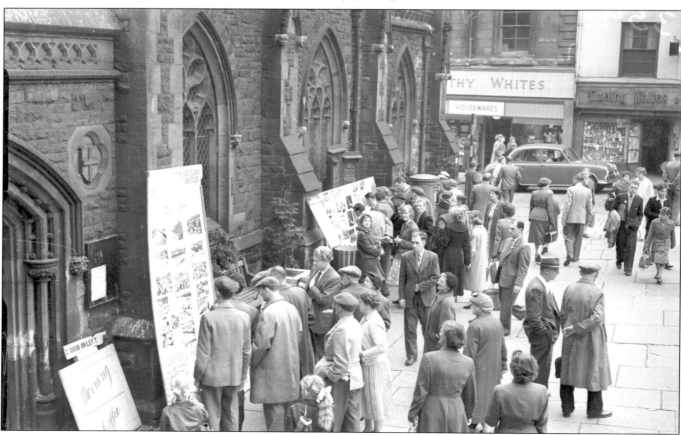

D o not mention old man's marbles to any aficionado of the bowling green; that description is the ultimate insult. Anyway, the game is more than just a simple pastime because it is steeped in the historical folklore of our past, as any schoolboy will tell you. If it was important enough for Francis Drake to attend to when the Spanish Armada hove into view, then it should be good enough for the rest of us. On 27 April 1951, with many of the players dressed in traditional bowling garb, the woods whizzed merrily across the greensward in front of Vane Tempest Hall. Situated on Maynard's Row, behind the Queen's Head public house on the corner of Sunderland Road and Sherburn Road where they meet to form the start of Gilesgate, this fine old house that overlooks the green is still standing. It had been one of the properties owned by the 3rd Marquess of Londonderry (1778-1854), the 'man on the horse' in Market Place. In 1819 he married the Irish heiress Frances Anne Vane-Tempest and the Marquess included her surname within his own. Unlike her husband, Frances was a popular figure, especially with the mining community as she funded fetes for them and recommended the setting up of pensions and retirement homes. It is appropriate that the house became the headquarters for the Gilesgate Community and Welfare Association. Vane Tempest Bowling Club members continue to enjoy practising their thumb tack and finger bias on the green today.

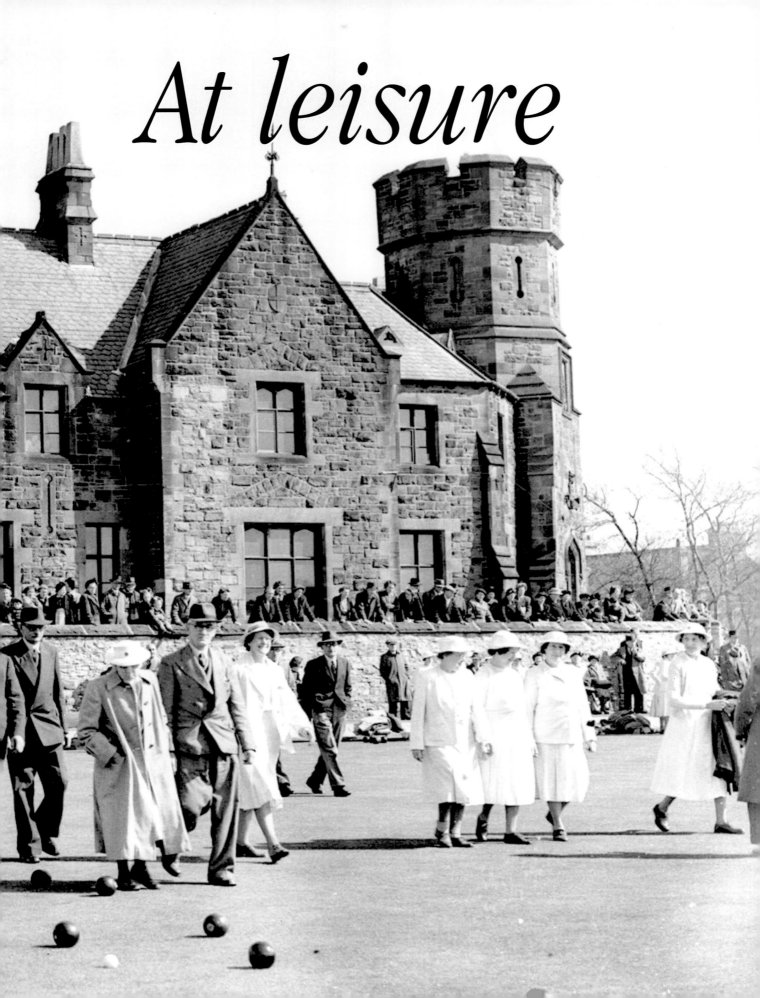

At leisure

Above: It is hard to believe that we are looking at the site of a shopping centre. These playing fields, belonging to Durham High School and originally part of Paradise Gardens, presented a tranquil setting in May 1947. In the foreground, a small group of children enjoyed a game of 'ring a roses' or 'mulberry bush', while more energetic youngsters dashed around the tennis court pretending to be Fred Perry, Bunny Austin or Dorothy Round. That summer, they would have plenty of time to enjoy their sport as the sun shone gloriously, making up for one of the worst winters in living memory. That was the season when the 'Middlesex twins', Bill Edrich and Denis Compton, each scored well over 3,000 runs apiece in a cricket season never to be rivalled for crowds, sunshine and strokeplay. It was also when Christian Dior introduced his 'new look' in women's fashion, which was all to the good if you had enough clothing coupons to buy his creation with its concentration on an hourglass figure. Much of the playing field has now been taken over by the Prince Bishops Shopping Centre. Happily, modern architects did not fall into the trap that lured their colleagues in the 1970s into creating concrete behemoths that blighted the horizon of many city centres. They eschewed the high rise and went in for a more attractive lower level design that blended better with the surrounding streets.

Below: This might have been lifted from a Christmas card or a chocolate box. An artist would give his eyeteeth to be able to pose such a scene, but this was all perfectly natural and shows how well photography is its own art form. The image is from six decades ago, but stands the test of time as a delightful picture that could fit into several categories. It is a wonderful riverside scene or might be one of a pretty woodland. Additionally, we could classify it as a British winter shot or one for a family album. In any collection, this would stand out as one of the best. It was taken in February 1947 on the Wearside footpath below Pelaw Wood, near the old ash tree that marked the starting point for races during Durham Regatta. Mrs HM Webster and her daughter, Hilary, were enjoying the crispness and freshness of the great outdoors during what was actually one of the harshest winters of the last century. Heavy snowstorms and sub-zero temperatures together with with a serious fuel shortage combined to bring the country to its economic knees. Coal trains could not get through 20 foot high snowdrifts and thousands of homes went without heating of lighting for long periods. Does little Hilary recall those times as she makes her way to the post office for her pension today? She will surely have some memory of racing down the snow covered slopes, sitting on an old tin tray, towards a snowman with buttons for eyes, a carrot for a nose and grandad's pipe sticking out of its face.

Below: Transport fascinated little lads in the middle years of the 20th century. They were never happier than playing with their Hornby train sets, powered by a transformer attached to the mains, whizzing Dinky racing cars around a circuit created in between the sitting room chairs and messing about with steam engines that used methylated spirit. They built moving cranes from Meccano and played happily for hours with tiny pots of paint, transfers, glue and bits of plastic snapped from larger pieces in their Airfix kits. In the 1950s they put together models of Spitfires and Hurricanes that their fathers had told them about or were inspired to create after reading about the exploits of Biggles or real heroes, such as Douglas Bader and Johnny Johnson. Many were the bedroom ceilings that had old monoplanes hanging down on strings that drove mum mad as she ducked every time she came in to change the bed or do the dusting, but woe betide her if she snagged one of her son's precious creations. Serious model makers graduated to membership of clubs dedicated to producing accurate scale reproductions of gliders, fighters, bombers and airliners. Norman Davis, at 13, was the youngest member of Durham Model Flying club. In January 1952 he showed off his prowess at an exhibition mounted at the Palladium Cinema, Claypath. The other lads stood open-mouthed as Norman explained the intricacies of his art.

Above: Some bikers in the 1950s and early 1960s developed and even revelled in a reputation for speed, danger and rowdy behaviour. Meeting up in rough, down at heel cafés and playing Gene Vincent music on the jukeboxes, they slicked back their Brylcreemed hair and preened their sideburns as girls with dirty fingernails drooled over them. They revved their engines and roared off into the night intent on burning up the highway, appearing to have the sort of death wish that inspired the Shangri Las to sing about the 'Leader of the pack' or Twinkle to warble an epitaph to the black-leathered 'Terry'. Chapters of Hell's Angels were a fearsome sight to ordinary Jills and Joes of the general public. Bank holidays at the seaside became battle-grounds when Mods on scooters and Rockers on motorbikes faced one another, both sides intent on creating mayhem. The image of two-wheeled motoring was sadly tarnished for such law abiding groups as the Durham City Motor Cycle Club, formed not long before this photograph was taken in September 1959. Their interests were in testing their skills and seeing the countryside, rather than punching the lights out of anyone who crossed them. These keen riders were about to embark on their first road trial. Bob Fletcher held the prize cup that he was donating for the winners of the 125 mile test. Bob was the landlord at the Volunteer Arms, Gilesgate and later presented the trophy to Ian Carr of Spennymoor and his navigator, John Robinson of Sacriston.

Below: This idyllic scene of Durham at play on The Racecourse was taken from a vantage point on the edge of Pelaw Wood on 26 May 1956. In the distance, we can just make out the old iron bridge that served Elvet Railway Station, but the photograph is dominated by the range of sports being played. 'Flanelled fools', as cricketers were once unkindly called, practised their art of leg glances and off cutters alongside tennis players hoping to be the next Angela Buxton, the Liverpool girl who reached the Wimbledon singles' final and won the doubles with Althea Gibson later that summer. To the right, woods, made from lignum vitae, skidded across the turf of the bowling green on their way to nestle alongside the jack, while walkers strolled along the river bank or watched a coxed four pull its way along the Wear. At the Olympic Games in Melbourne, held in December, our rowers would come home without a single medal of any colour as we had no Redgrave or Pinsent around in those days. The Racecourse covers 20 acres and now includes four football pitches, a first class county standard cricket ground, a rugby pitch, plus two fives and two squash courts in the Pavilion. It was the previous home of Durham County Cricket Club before its move to the Riverside, Chester-le-Street. In recent year it has also hosted the Great North International Cross Country races.

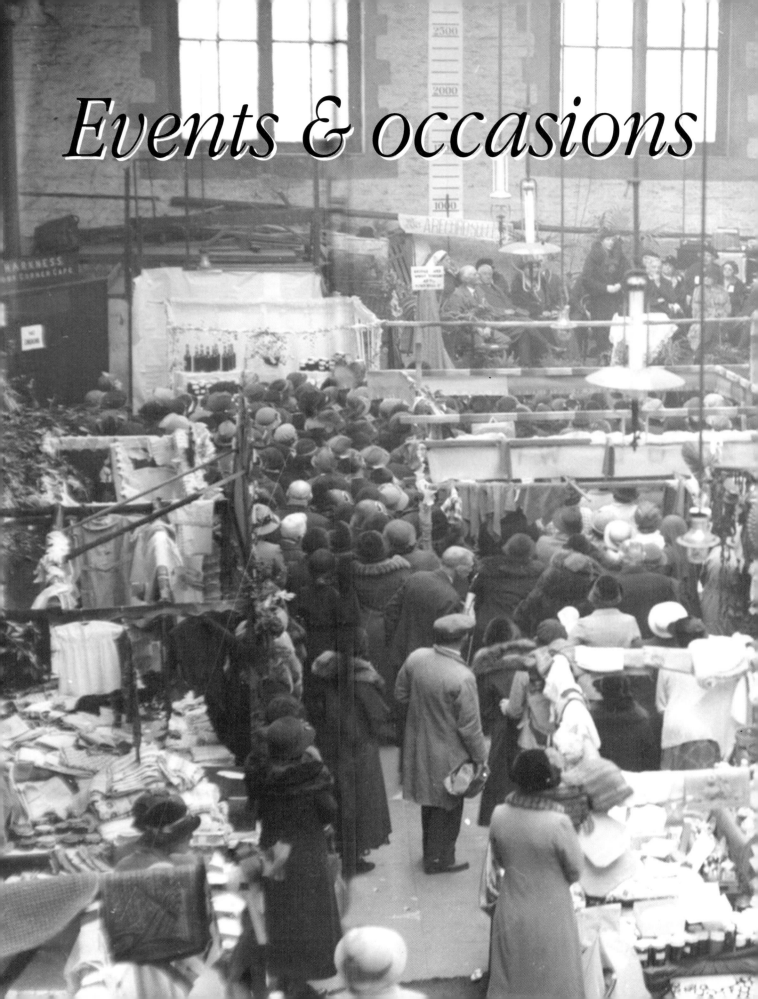

Events & occasions

The indoor market was established in 1851 and, entered from Market Place or by climbing the steps from Back Silver Street, provides an airy and atmospheric setting for some 70 or 80 stalls. On 22 October 1935 it played host to the Durham County Hospital bazaar and the honoured guests included Lady Surtees, Dean Allington and Dr Gordon, Bishop of Jarrow. The hospital was built in 1853 on an elevated point and was described in literature of the time as being a 'spacious building of stone in the Elizabethan style'. With room initially for 44 patients, it was built at a cost of £7,500, supported by donations and public subscriptions. In 1867 male and female convalescent wards were added at a cost of £2,400 as a memorial to Dean Waddington, who in 1865 contributed £2,000 to the funds of the hospital and subsequently a further sum of £2,000. This generous benefactor then bequeathed by will some £6,000 more. John Eden of Beamish Park, who gave a sum of £2,000 towards their creation and eventually willed another £10,000, added additional wards. These were opened on 2 December 1886, thus making room for about 60 patients. By the date of this bazaar, the hospital had grown considerably in size but still needed to attract further funding. The crowds in the market hall should have helped swell the coffers, but the shoppers did not have much cash to spare and the presence of the Bishop was poignant as unemployed workers from his town would make their famous march to London just 12 months later.

Below: Britain became almost paranoid about physical fitness in the 1930s. Health and beauty clubs and open air exercise groups were all the rage. Running on the spot, jumps astride, press-ups, touching toes and all manner of physical jerks were seen as a panacea for our accumulated cobwebs. Of course it did not matter that, after a session of swinging Indian clubs or performing ribbon waving routines to music, we lit up a Woodbine and went off for a pint of Vaux. The crowd that gathered at the city cricket ground on the Racecourse had not come to listen to miners' speeches or to applaud anyone's cover drive. Somewhat belatedly, as the main event took place in May, this physical fitness display was put on as part of the coronation celebrations on 16 July 1937. By then, George VI was well used to the crown given to him by Archbishop Cosmo Lang. That did not trouble the spectators who were either proud parents or men pretending to be followers of gymnastics, but in truth looked forward to seeing young women in short skirts. On the right, on the far side of the old Durham Gardens we can just spot the Pineapple Inn. It was a Durham landmark that was, by the early 19th century, well established as a public house. However, in 1926 the pub lost its licence to sell alcohol. The gardens are shown as having a bowling green in the first Ordnance Survey map of 1857 and recreational activities continued to be a feature even after the sale of much of the land to the Hopps family at the end of World War I. Part of the estate was later acquired by St Hild's College and, in 1985, Richard Hopps and the college both sold pieces of their holdings to the council so that restoration of the gardens could take place.

Right: Remember when we had an empire? If so, you must belong to a mature group of readers because the term was being phased out as long ago as 1931 when the British Commonwealth of Nations was formed. However, this organi-sation represented former dependencies that wanted to maintain links with the old country and the British Empire still existed as we retained sovereignty over numerous colonies, protectorates and assorted territories. Even as late as 1958 Cardiff still referred to the sporting occasion it hosted as the Empire Games, even though the term 'Commonwealth' had been added some years before. Independence for India, Burma and Ceylon, along with the creation of Pakistan, in the late 1940s began the movement towards abandonment of the use of 'Empire' and it was largely put to bed in the 1950s and early 1960s as former African and Caribbean colonies gained their freedom. But, on 24 May 1937 we were still celebrating Empire Day as an occasion when we could revel in the influence and standing that we believed our nation enjoyed. The date had special significance, being Queen Victoria's birthday. The Bluecoat School, Claypath had held its own festivities since 1933 and 10 year old Joan Francis was the latest in the line of pretty May Queens, here led out by heralds prior to her coronation. How proud her mum must have been and how jealous the mothers of her classmates, though they tried not to show that they were possessed by a green-eyed monster.

Above right: Bigwigs just love to be involved in the unveiling of statues, the launching of ships or the blessing of some new place of worship. They are even

happy to be snapped cutting the ceremonial ribbon at more mundane events. Situated not far from where shards of broken glass from Watson and Wood's 'pop' factory could often be found, the occasion on 12 April 1938 that brought VIPs from their offices was the opening of the 'Silver link' footbridge at Gilesgate. Designed by the City Engineer, Mr JW Green, it provided a connection with Pelaw Wood. Alderman JTE Dickeson, on the left, was the man entrusted with the scissors, though the Mayor, Councillor WE Bradley, resplendent in his chain of office, kept a watchful eye on the proceedings at his side. The bridge was built by the Cleveland Bridge Company of Darlington and is said to have been inspired by the one that crossed Victoria Falls on the Zambezi. Local wags moved locations a little when they pretended to be Livingstone and Stanley as they 'presumed' to restage their meeting. However, the city felt that the erection of the bridge required marking as being of significance and a model of it was put on permanent display in the town hall.

Right: In 1939, not long before 'the day that war broke out', as Rob Wilton might have described it, parents, pupils, governors and dignitaries connected with one of Britain's foremost public schools were gathered together at the naming ceremony for the locomotive 'Durham School'. Situated close to the city centre, within earshot of the cathedral bells, Durham School, refounded by Cardinal Langley in 1414 and again by Henry VIII in 1541, has a long tradition of excellence. The vast majority of its pupils go on to universities, but while at the school they are still just youngsters, after all. This was demonstrated by some of the boys listening to the boring speeches coming from the platform, when all they wanted to do was rush off and see a steam locomotive in the raw. They can be forgiven for not paying attention, because there was no competition between dry oratory and the excitement of one of Sir Nigel Gresley's creations. The only time that the lads listened hard on such an occasion as this or during an official Speech Day was when they heard the words 'half day's holiday'. Male domination was broken in 1985 when girls were admitted to the sixth form and inaugurated Pimlico House, named after the street where it is situated. The school became fully co-educational in 1999, though its 100 girls work in a single sex haven within a co-educational establishment under the beady eye of housemistress, Lucy Hewitt.

Below: The boys from Durham School threw their boaters into the air to celebrate the naming of a locomotive after their educational establishment. The headmaster, Reverend HK Luce, received a memorial replica nameplate from the chairman of London and North Eastern Railways (LNER), Sir William Gray. The ceremony took place at Elvet Railway Station on 15 June 1939. The V2 4-6-0 locomotive, resplendent in its apple green livery, was one of 184 of this class to be built, though only eight were ever afforded a name. The V2s were LNER's most famous mixed traffic designs and among the most successful that Sir Nigel Gresley ever built. This class of locomotive was allocated to all regions of the LNER, though most were posted to sheds along the East Coast Main Line between Kings Cross and Aberdeen. The first one, 'Green Arrow' quickly became famous working the first leg of the King's Cross to Glasgow express goods run. During World War II, the V2s worked many heavy passenger trains. 'Durham School' was built in May 1939, being the second and the last to be named for a northern school. St Peter's, York was the first. Built in March 1939, it continued in service until June 1965. No 4831, 'Durham School', was manned here by Bob Hodgson and John Breeze, both sadly killed on active service in France. This locomotive was deemed obsolete in October 1962.

Many wearing that symbol of the northern working man, the cloth cap, demonstrated their solidarity with one another under the symbolic miners' banner in the 1935 march along Elvet. This was during the latter end of the depression years that had seen unemployment rise to 3 million, families wondering where on earth their next meal would come from and bitter resentment against an establishment that either did not care or was impotent to do anything that would alleviate the suffering. It was no wonder that the ill feeling spilled over into rioting in some instances. Hannen Swaffer (1879-1962), one of the speakers at this year's gala, was a notable supporter of the miners' lot. A left wing firebrand, he worked as a journalist for the Daily Herald and supported their cause in print and in person. A complex man, he also worked as a drama critic and developed a keen commitment to spiritualism. After the 1935 gala he presented an album of photographs of the occasion to the Miners' Association, captioning this picture with a critical comment on the cathedral's right wing establishment. The significance of the 'big meeting' was illustrated by the presence on the speakers' platform of Sir Stafford Cripps (1889-1952), Herbert Morrison (1888-1965) and George Lansbury (1859-1940), all major Labour party figures keen to address a crowd of an estimated 150,000 on the Racecourse.

When the war ended in 1945 the jubilation on the streets is hard to imagine. VE Day, when we celebrated the victory in Europe, was a scene of unbridled emotion. Huge crowds gathered in town and city centres and impromptu congas were danced along the streets. Complete strangers hugged one another and soldiers home on leave were startled to be kissed by women old enough to be their grannies. Mums, in their homes, used up a week's butter, dried egg, flour and sugar rations to bake a real cake and share it with neighbours as everyone pulled together to have the finest street party of their lives. Just for a while, they forgot the privations of the previous six years and that every family knew

someone who would not be coming home. It was a time to thank God and Mr Churchill. The bluebirds were flying across the Wear as much as those white cliffs down south. When the war with Japan ended three months later, there was more partying, but nothing like the sheer joy and relief that was demonstrated in early May. To mark the anniversary of the ending of hostili-ties, Durham City Corporation held a party in the Indoor Market for 500 pensioners. The Mayor, Councillor JL Robson greeted the guests and invited them to enjoy an evening's entertainment after they had finished their celebratory tea. They sang 'We'll meet again', but hoped never to have to do so again, because they had experienced the horrors of two world wars.

Below: Looking across Market Place today is not dissimilar from the view we had just after the war. Not only are most of the buildings as they were, with a few exceptions, but many of the major businesses remain. Notable among these are the banking institutions, such as National Westminster, or NatWest, the Midland and Barclays. What has changed is the way they operate. A lot of people no longer go in through the doors, merely using the automatic cash dispensers in the wall for their funds. Barclays pioneered this method of extracting money as far back as 1967, though the idea was slow to take off. However, by the late 1980s as we all began using credit cards with greater freedom, the notion of using a cash card became more obvious. By the start of this century cheques had become almost obsolete, with a book lasting for a year or more, instead of needing replacing every couple of months. There are some drawbacks and we have lost the personal touch of direct involvement with cashiers and bank managers we knew. It is now impossible, in most cases, to make telephone contact with a bank directly. Instead, we deal with a dreaded call centre, based anywhere from Manchester to Mumbai, with the additional annoyance of pressing one to do this, two to do that and three to get cut off. This photograph dates from 26 July 1947 when the Thornley section was but one of those making their way past the old police box to listen to speeches on The Racecourse during the miners' gala.

Above: FW Woolworth opened its store at 17 Market Place in the 1920s on the site of the former Rose and Crown Hotel that was once owned by Sir John Duck, the 17th century butcher, colliery and property owner who is sometimes referred to as Durham's Dick Whittington. His house was opposite the present Woolworth's site. The Rose and Crown passed into the hands of the Tempest family in 1710. Miners and their families from Crook Drift, also known as the 'Hole in the Wall' colliery, created the hubbub outside Woolworth's. They were moving out along Silver Street on 23 July 1949 at a time when coalmining had just undergone a significant change. In July 1945, Labour swept to power as the electorate stated that it wanted no more of the old guard that had taken it into a six year war that cost so much in lives and livelihood. Clement Attlee was the new man in Downing Street and his cabinet embarked on a series of reforms that would radically alter the fabric of British society. The new government brought in the National Health Service, free secondary education for all up to the age of 15 and proposed nationalisation for many of our industries, including iron and steel, road haulage, gas and electricity, the ports and railways. On New Year's Day 1947 flags were hoisted at Britain's pits, proclaiming new ownership by the state. However miners, though hateful of capitalist colliery owners, were unconvinced about the merits of those running the National Coal Board.

Above: We pay our taxes, but there are still occasions when we are expected to dip into our pockets for some other cause that, perhaps, the council or the government should be funding. In what the Tories would later refer to as a 'double whammy', we are often caught out twice over. Workers pay income tax on their wages and then again on any profit made from investments. Another form of stealth tax is the one whereby people are expected to contribute via public subscription. All these crafty ways of bleeding us drier than ever are nothing new. Churches, town halls, statues, memorials etc have, for centuries, often relied on the man in the street chipping in to provide the funds for Britain's major edifices. In May 1954, a bazaar in the Indoor market was in full swing. It was organised as part of the fund raising activities for the restoration of Prebends Bridge. Nicholson started its erection in 1772 and it took six years to complete. The bridge, named after the prebends or canons of the cathedral, replaced earlier wooden and then stone bridges that earlier stood on the site. It is located at a truly pretty spot that affords beautiful views along the river and has inspired poets and artists, including Walter Scott and Joseph Turner, to produce memorable lines and paintings. The area around Prebends Bridge is sometimes called 'Count's Corner', being the spot where the dwarf, Count Boruwlaski, came to live in the late 18th century.

Top right: It was not only miners that held 'big meetings'. This was the one held in 1960 when members of the Methodist churches got together for their own version at Durham Cathedral, with a congregation of about 2,000. Three strands of Methodism were to be found in Durham, with the first belonging to Wesleyans who were established here in 1743. They converted a building on Rotten Row in 1770, rebuilding it in Old Elvet in 1808. The Primitive Methodist Chapel functioned during 1825-62 behind 33 Silver Street and the New Connexion was set up in Old Elvet in 1829, before moving to the Bethel Chapel, North Road in 1853. The miners' 'big meetings' and religion will forever be linked by the incident in 1925 that still brings a smile to the face long after all the participants have passed away. Feelings generally were running high as unemployment was on the rise and wages were poor in the year leading up to the general strike 12 months later. The church was seen as being part of the establishment, so its standing as a friend of the working classes was at something of an all time low. The Bishop of Durham, Herbert Hensley Henson, was a vociferous critic of the miners and strike action in particular, a practice he felt should be outlawed. After some five years of his reactionary views being heard on a regular basis, some people attending the 1925 gala thought they had spotted the Bishop and promptly attempted to throw him into the river. Unfortunately, it was a case of mistaken identity and the Dean of Durham, Dr J Weldon, was the recipient of the manhandling. He had come to lecture on the evils of drink and found himself in it instead!

Above: The Shakespeare Band marched past the Dunelm Hotel, with its leader, Mr R Clark, striding out proudly, with Sherburn Road's John Mollom to the left. Brass bands are a great feature of northern life. Every colliery and village had its own that practised assiduously and it is a wonderful tribute to the adaptability of the band members that many of them could work underground in a tough environment and still produce music of a delicate nature, in addition to the rousing tunes they also played. 'Brassed off', a 1996 movie starring Pete Postlethwaite, was a moving, if simple drama about a mining community facing the closure of its pit as it struggled to keep the band going and win a national competition. It may have been tosh to some, but those who had similar experiences could identify with some of the elements of the film. On 18 July 1959, the speakers at the miners' gala included W Paynter, the general secretary of the National Union of Mineworkers. He was accompanied by three members of Parliament, A Blenkinsop, CP Mayhew and Aneurin Bevan, that fine orator from the Welsh valleys known to friends and foes as 'Nye'. This ex miner became Minister for Health in 1945 and steered the setting up of the National Health Service. Sadly, he died at the age of 62 less than a year after attending this rally.

Below: At first glance, this may not seem much. It appears to be just any other children's party, with a few homemade hats, hooters and a couple of boxes of fancy cakes and a plate of sandwiches. But, the date is significant. Looking carefully at the headgear sported by some of the children reveals that they are wearing crowns. This was 2 June 1953 and the day was celebrated across the country with the sort of enthusiasm we had not experienced since the end of the war. Many thought that we were now about to embark on a new Elizabethan age, thanks to the presence of a young monarch at Buckingham Palace who seemed to herald that the austere postwar years were coming to an end. Prosperity and a golden future were just around the corner, or so we hoped. The portents were good. Colonel John Hunt led an expedition that conquered Everest, POWs were on their way back from Korea, Joe Stalin was dead and Stanley Matthews had won his FA Cupwinner's medal at last. To cap it all, the Queen was, at this very moment, making her way into Westminster Abbey for the only coronation ceremony Britain would see during the second half of the 20th century. Flags, bunting and streamers flew all over Britain as village halls and inner city streets all hosted parties in honour of the special day. This one took place at Gilesgate Welfare Centre, Vane Tempest Hall.

Above: On 20 November 1869 Durham Miners' Association held its first meeting at the Market Hotel and, from this inaugural occasion, the idea of the miners' gala was born. Open to all members working in the county's coalfields, the first gathering, known colloquially as 'the big meeting', was held at Wharton Park on 12 August 1871. Some 5,000 men and their families turned up to what was to become an annual institution, attracting hundreds of thousands in its heyday. The gala was held at the Racecourse the following year and has continued there ever since, with a few exceptions mainly due to meetings being suspended during wartime. It became a focal point for the British Labour movement, being the largest gathering and demonstration held on a regular basis for the working classes. The tradition of using the third Saturday in July was soon established and socialist politicians pencilled the date into their diaries as a 'must do' each year. So large did the crowds become after the second world war that two platforms had to be erected for speakers to use. George Brown, Harold Wilson, Michael Foot and Tony Benn became regulars in the 1950s and 1960s. In this scene, the Washington 'F' Pit Lodge proudly displayed its banner on leaving the cathedral following a service there.

Esh - winning

The year 2003 saw £3 million being invested in an eight acre site at Bowburn to provide new, purpose built headquarters, yards, workshops and maintenance facilities which enabled the core of each business in the Esh Group of companies to relocate onto one site.

The Group was originally formed in 1999, following the merger of a number of like minded companies, all based near the village of Esh Winning, County Durham.

Deerness Fencing and Lumsden & Carroll formed Dunelm Castle Homes in 1995.

That joint venture led to further collaborations. A formal partnering arrangement was entered into in 1999: a holding company was established, individual company shares were exchanged and the Esh Group was created.

The next addition to the Esh Group was Sones, a landscaping company. Sones was facing severe financial difficulties, due to the failure of a major contract, and despite all efforts the company was taken into receivership. The Esh Group negotiated with the receiver to purchase some of the assets of the company, saving not only jobs but also retaining many existing contracts.

Electrical Contractors, Bartram, joined the Group shortly afterwards, providing the opportunity to develop specific building services expertise within the Group. Robson Walker, Electrical and Street Lighting Contractors, joined the Group in 2001 and merged with Bartram the following year.

As the number of staff employed in the Esh Group continued to grow, a specialist training division, North East Construction Training (NECT), was established within the Group. NECT trains not only Esh Group employees, but also employees of many other construction companies in the North East.

Dunelm Property Services was formed in 2002, to build, regenerate and repair property in the social housing sector.

Also formed in 2002, was Mechplant (North East) Limited. This business provides a plant and equipment hire service to Esh Group companies, as well as to an extensive list of external clients.

The latest company, Bardon Esh, a joint venture between the Esh Group and Aggregate Industries, a multi national corporation, is a waste management & recycling business. The Group feels that as the nature of the work that it carries out has an impact on the environment, it should do all that it can to help protect our valuable natural resources. Through the formation of this joint venture company, the Group believes that it can make a positive contribution to environmental and sustainability issues.

The Esh Group has extended its business interests beyond construction to acquire a controlling interest in Tursdale and Philadelphia Business Parks, as well as wholly owning Tanfield Lea Industrial Park.

But what were are the origins of today's multi-million pound enterprise organisation that employs over 700 people?

Jack Lumsden was born and bred in Esh Winning. At the age of 15, he had started work at Waterhouse Colliery. In 1967 the colliery closed and Jack went to work for the Water Board, and for various construction companies. In 1968 whilst working for Tarmac, Jack met his future business partner and lifelong friend, Tony Carroll, who also worked there.

Tony Carroll was born in Tipperary, Ireland. Whilst working in London, he met his future wife, Anne, and moved to Esh Winning.

In 1971, work at Tarmac was declining. Over a drink in the Newhouse Club in Esh Winning, Jack and Tony decided to join forces to become the partnership Lumsden & Carroll.

***Top:** Founders, Jack Lumsden (left) and Tony Carroll.*
***Right:** Lumsden and Carroll's old office, 65 Durham Road, Esh Winning.*

Tony Carroll had a contact in Jim Hastings, who had his own company. In 1972, Jim Hastings gave Lumsden & Carroll its first job at Bede Industrial Estate in Jarrow, where Jack and Tony subcontracted to lay a pipeline.

At first, Jack and Tony, carrying shovel and pick, used local buses to get to work. Agreeing that there was a need for some mode of transport, they employed local man Fred Gressmann, as he was one of the few in the village who could drive, and had a car.

Fred Gressmann would subsequently work his way up in the Company to become Construction Director of Lumsden & Carroll, and later become Engineering Director of Dunelm Castle Homes.

Shortly after employing Fred, with his blue Sunbeam Rapier, the workload grew and the small firm employed more local people, including Michael Barrigan, Colin Davison, John Hennigan and Derek Rayner. All are still with the company more than three decades later.

In 1974 a red, white and blue Bedford van was bought for £95. The reason they later chose green, as the corporate company colour, was because when they went and bought their first brand new van, a green one stood out from the rest. Even today, the green coloured fleet of vehicles is instantly recognisable as Lumsden & Carroll.

Three years later, in 1977, Jack and Tony bought their first excavator, a second hand Whitlock for what was then a fortune at £2,500. This was a real turning point for the business.

At first, the firm's office was simply a room in Jack Lumsden's house. There in this 'office', pricing was done in the evenings and wages were done at the weekend.

A typical day involved getting up at 5am, to start work an hour later, both Jack and Tony would each work a 12 hour day. Tony Carroll, however, would often turn his watch back a couple of hours so that the lads would work even longer. 'What time is it Tony?' they would ask. 'Three o'clock', he would

reply, when it was actually 5pm. It was this determined attitude to get the job done that formed the core resolve of Lumsden & Carroll and set the agenda for what was to come.

Tony Carroll had, and still has, that Irish charm (remember Victor McLaglan?) that would work on anyone and could bring the birds down from the trees. On one occasion, when he and employee Paul James were driving to work, they (Tony) crashed into the rear of a Jaguar. Initially, the owner of the Jaguar was furious, but once Tony had spoken with the man, he not only agreed to give the two of them a lift to their site, so they could do their day's work, but even loaded up their wheelbarrow into the boot of his Jaguar!

Another early member of the team, John Hennigan, then started work for Lumsden & Carroll at Mattison's Meats in Dragonville, Durham, working evenings, weekends and factory holidays. He had started on a two week contract but is still with Lumsden & Carroll after nearly thirty years!!! (As an aside, in 1997, on one of the Northumbrian Water sites, John Hennigan and colleague, Richard Potts, saved two boys from drowning in the River Tees and they were both hailed as heroes. On another of his sites, during restoration work on Myton Bridge, in North Yorkshire, John Hennigan found an unexploded bomb and had to call the Bomb Disposal Team!)

Turning back the clock, the first staff Christmas party was held at the Board Inn, Langley Park. Eight people were

there, each of them getting six pints and chicken and chips, with the bill coming to £17- 10 shillings. In 2003, over 400 people attended the Christmas Party, and the bill was considerably more than £17-10!.

Back in the early days, however, Tony would go round to Jack's house after work to discuss the day, as they had often been on different sites. Then they would plan the next day or week's work. They'd also discuss Esh Winning Football Club, which the pair began supporting in 1977.

Once the workforce reached 15, or so, Jack became office-based, while Tony specialised in the site management side of the business.

Lumsden & Carroll's first engineer arrived in 1978, in the shape of John Hayton; until then John had worked for Durham County Council.

That same year, a yard was bought at West Terrace from the Coal Board. The firm moved on to the site there in 1980, following a fight and considerable discussion with the local authorities. Lumsden & Carroll received a lot of support from the local MP for Wear Valley District, Ernest Armstrong.

Meanwhile back in 1984, Jack and Tony bought their first office at 65/66 Durham Road, Esh Winning. In the mid 1990s it would be extended into 64 Durham Road.

The next big turning point of the development of Lumsden & Carroll was the introduction of Brian Manning to the company in 1990. Tony Carroll had worked for many years on site with Brian Manning, a Contracts Manager for Monk Civil Engineering. Brian had been described as 'a raging red bull standing in a field'. Tony and Jack saw this enthusiasm, the flair he had for numbers, and his potential to take their business forward.

One of the first moves Brian Manning instigated was a joint venture with Dunelm Homes (now Dunelm Castle Homes), then a subsidiary of Deerness Fencing.

Why was it that Lumsden & Carroll succeeded when so many similar ventures failed? Why did they never have a year without making a profit? Was it because they offered a 24 hour call out service seven days a week? Was it because no job was ever deemed to be impossible?
Was it because they were committed to completing every job on time and to budget? Was it because Customer Care was paramount?.

According to Jack and Tony, the combination of the Lumsden 'brain' and the Carroll 'brawn' provided exactly

Below: *A Lumsden and Carroll Group photograph with Jack Lumsden and Tony Carroll behind top, June 1991.*

the right balance in the recipe for stubbornness and ambition. 'We fought from dawn til dark', recalls Tony Carroll. 'There's no such word as can't', says Jack Lumsden.

But Lumsden & Carroll and Dunelm Castle Homes are not the only original components of the Esh Group.

In 1976, after working for his father as a landscaper, Bill Sones formed his own company, WW Sones Junior Ltd. He started trading from a back lane in the small village of Langley Moor. Within a short space of time, he realised that in order to expand he would need a depot facility and extra labour. In talks with Brandon UDC, he learned that the council was building an extension road into Littleburn Industrial Estate.

He rented a half an acre site on Littleburn Industrial Estate, with a five year option to buy the land for £1,175, and within four years he had completed the purchase of it.

Bill Sones' first goals were to have no debts, a new car and a commercial vehicle within five years. By working non-stop, doing all private work, he achieved his goals.

One of Bill's first contracts was for Leech Homes at Newton Hall, doing one garden a day.

Bill then obtained more business by calling at the doors of already completed houses, asking owners if they liked his workmanship, and asking if they would like their gardens maintained.

Bill was one of the first people in the area to own a Stihl Saw: a power mechanical saw for cutting flags. Bill was also well ahead of his competitors in owning the first Bobcat skid steer loading shovel in the North East. The first large contracts he secured were to renovate Cornthwaite Park in Whitburn, and to carry out landscaping for Coulson Estates at Langley Moor. Bill also introduced a new transportation system to get the lads to work: a second hand double decker bus - and he was the driver!

During these early years, Bill established a good working relationship as a subcontractor with Michael Hogan of Deerness Fencing.

After eight years of successful trading, Bill Sones put down his tools to become office based. Long term employees, who are still with the company today, include Darren Hardman, Jim Campbell and David Smith who all started out as grass cutters, but subsequently progressed to managerial and supervisory roles.

In subsequent years, the business had its ups and downs. Sones did all the construction work at the Metro Centre, but it lost cash in one year to three separate

Top: *John Hayton of Lumsden and Carroll receives Quality Assurance accreditation from Sir Michael Latham, 21st May 1996.*

fencing industry as a labour only sub contractor. This was with his two cousins, John and James Duffy.

In 1976, Michael, John and James Duffy formed Deerness Fencing Company based at Newhouse Farm, which was then the home of John Duffy. Michael managed and worked tirelessly to make Deerness Fencing grow. By 1985, when the Duffy brothers retired and Deerness Fencing was a registered limited company, annual turnover had reached £750,000. The company had built up a workforce of approximately 50 people, some of whom still work in the company today.

In 1984, Michael began to build stone houses on land bought from his father's family estate. The company was called Dunelm Homes Ltd, and Michael was assisted by Gerry Close and later Seamus Slevin, as Accountant. The company built up a reputation over the next 10 years as builders of quality stone houses, with an annual turnover of approximately £2million. This company continues today outside of the Group, but has refocused on commercial property and land. The expertise of Gerry and Seamus was still retained by Michael for his other business activities up until a few months ago.

Some of the long term staff have moved on or retired from Deerness Fencing, notably: Rita Hogan, Tony Claughan and Dermot Slevin.

firms, which all went into receivership within weeks of each other, costing the company £170,000. If it had not been for the good working relationship with its main supplier, Johnsons of Whixley, then WW Sones would have suffered much worse. The firm is still trading with Johnsons today.

According to Bill Sones, 'When I had my own company, I felt a sense of pride and responsibility, knowing that all these people relied on Bill Sones operating that day'.

Sadly, due to a problematical contract in Scotland, WW Sones Jnr Ltd was forced into receivership in October 1999.

It was then that Lumsden & Carroll bought out the maintenance section of the company, the larger part of the business, from the Receiver and named the new company Sones Maintenance and Environmental Ltd. Bill Sones then took the opportunity to retire.

Long before he started Deerness Fencing, Michael Hogan was one of the youngest students to go to Houghall College. After leaving Houghall, he worked on his father's farm in Cornsay Colliery, which also doubled as a pub called The Fir Tree, known locally as The Monkey's Nest.

Michael decided that farming wasn't for him, and went to work for Wimpey. By the time he was 24, he had worked for two dozen employers but never settled in anything. It was then that Michael went into forestry and haulage for 18 months, and then into the

Top: The first job carried out by Deerness Fencing at Bowes Railway Incline.
Right: The first Deerness Fencing company social gathering at Lumley Castle.

Deerness Fencing was based at Newhouse Farm, Esh Winning until 2003 when when it joined the other Esh Group Companies at its the new corporate headquarters in Bowburn.

Hard work, customer care and loyalty of employees have been the main reasons for the company's growth. Bob Wall, who joined the company in 1996, and has been Managing Director since 1999, has played an enormous role in taking the company forward to allow Michael Hogan to concentrate on Group activities.

Deerness Fencing prides itself on having many long term clients such as Yuill Homes, UK Coal and Local Authorities.

Michael Hogan knew Brian Manning before he had joined Lumsden & Carroll. Both knew that if they could combine the Lumsden & Carroll operation with Deerness Fencing and associated companies, a formidable force within the construction industry would emerge.

They formed many joint ventures before finally merging the companies as the Esh Group in 1999.

Michael Hogan became Chairman of the Esh Group in 1999, and retired in December 2003, leaving the company in the capable hands of the Executive Directors supported by the Non Executive Directors. Michael remains a non executive director and is retained by the group to assist the land and development teams.

The Esh Group was given the recognition that it rightly deserved by winning the Company of the Year title at the 2003 North East Business Awards. This prestigious award was made by a panel of judges representing a broad spectrum of the Regional Economy. What they saw in the Esh Group that led them to raise it above the other organisations that they considered was a dynamic, forward looking, service driven company that values all of its employees.

In addition to the Esh Group investment in its own employees, it has also sought to invest in the local community and help reduce the skills shortage in the construction industry. The Fit for Employment initiative, jointly developed with Deerness Valley Comprehensive School, is a scheme to expose young people to the wide and varied work environment that exists within the construction sector. It provides an insight into the various career opportunities within the industry, and delivers measurable skills that add value to each students Record of Achievement. The programme's ultimate benefit is the 20 Modern Apprenticeships per year that the Esh Group will give to those who successfully complete the programme. The Fit for Employment initiative has received regional and national recognition for its innovative approach and real contribution to employment. This recognition has resulted in the programme achieving Pathfinder Status, awarded by the Department for Employment and Skills (DfES).

The continued prosperity of the Esh Group can only be achieved by the endeavours of its employees. The Group relies upon the continuous efforts of its management and personnel to optimise close co-operation through teamwork, effective communication, and to provide a friendly professional service. All of these essential factors assist the Esh Group to establish robust, long-term and beneficial relationships with its clients.

The Esh Group invests a great deal into the training and development of its employees. The Group has a comprehensive training programme that has been designed and developed for all grades and disciplines of personnel in each of the member companies. Employees are actively encouraged and financially supported to seek further qualifications and skills for their personal development and for the service delivery requirements of Esh Group clients.

The Esh Group continues to seek business opportunities that fit well with the core businesses of the existing Group companies, that enhance business synergies and that meet the cultural values upon which they have grown the organisation.

Reflecting on the growth of the Esh Group since its formation, who knows what's coming next?

Top: *From left to right: Michael Hogan, Jack Lumsden, Sir Bobby Robson and Tony Carroll pictured at the official opening of Esh Group's bespoke headquarters in Durham, 17th March 2004.*

On the home front

Below: In the late 1930s Britain was slow to acknowledge the threat posed by the activity of fascist forces across Europe and in northeast Africa. The warning signs were clear enough, but the government acted like an ostrich. It pinned its hopes on the negotiating skills of Prime Minister Chamberlain who thought he had gained 'peace for our time' when he returned from Munich in the autumn of 1938 waving a piece of paper signed by Adolf Hitler. He should have looked at the evidence elsewhere. Spain had been rocked by civil war since 1936, the same year that Italy annexed Abyssinia, and Germany marched into Austria in early 1938. Within a week of Chamberlain's futile declaration Hitler's troops jackbooted into Czechoslovakia. The threat of war now became real, even to the most optimistic in Britain. The Air Raid Precaution (ARP) service swung into action and civil defence bills were hurriedly rushed through parliament. In early 1939 the Home Office announced that thousands of air raid shelters were to be issued to Londoners and those in other vulnerable cities. Plans for evacuating children were made, gas masks issued and training given to enable civilians to respond to air raids and invasion. After war was declared in September 1939, men and women of the ARP doubled their efforts. Here, wardens treated mock casualties from the 5th Durham Scouts during an exercise in north Durham during December 1939.

Above: During World War I the general public became used to drives for salvaging waste and scrap that could be recycled into ordnance. There were also fund raising weeks mounted in town centres for money to help build warships and, towards the end of the hostilities, newfangled tanks. When the balloon went up again in 1939 it was not long before the same activities began all over again. This time, the efforts were even greater. In the 1914-18 war manpower was paramount, but the second world war placed as much emphasis on hardware as it did on personnel. This was a new type of confrontation where machines became precious commodities as battles were fought at much longer ranges and now included the skies in addition to land and sea. Durham Girl Guides, plus members of various girls' clubs, got together in July 1940 to do their bit for the war effort. They collected as much aluminium as they could. Seen near the ironmonger's of Fleming and Neil in Claypath, perhaps they had persuaded the shopkeeper to part with some of his stock. However, the girls mainly concentrated on encouraging householders to part with pots and pans that could help to turn out another Hurricane or Spitfire. The guides looked smart in their uniforms, but clothes' rationing meant that they had to make do with the same garments, even when they outgrew them. To preserve modesty, they tacked strips of spare material to their hemlines. It was all part of the make do and mend policy that the government promoted.

Above: 'Now, what's all this 'ere then, you 'orrible little man?' Possibly not, for Major General CL Loewen, commanding officer of the 50th Division, was no role model for the part played by Bill Fraser as Sergeant Major Claude Snudge in ITV's hugely successful 'Army Game', a late 1950s' send up of National Service. The series gave great opportunities to comedians and actors in supporting roles to go on to great success elsewhere. Ted Lune, Norman Rossington, Alfie Bass, Michael Medwin, Bernard Bresslaw, Frank Williams and Dick Emery all benefited from their time in this show. But, these members of the 8th Battalion Durham Light Infantry knew that there was a more serious side to soldiering in March 1948. They had a job to do, even if the second world war was now in the past. The world was still not a safe place as Russia started to flex its muscles and would soon blockade Berlin. The men lined up for inspection outside the Drill Hall at the bottom end of Gilesgate Bank. They were waiting for the arrival of Emmanuel Shinwell MP (1884-1986), then the Minister for War. Two officers and war heroes, Lieutenant Colonel GL Wood DSO MC and Captain PF Greenwood MC, were also in attendance when the fiery socialist politician came as part of his promotional tour of northern command. Shinwell, later to become Baron Shinwell of Easington, was encouraging staff officers to help the push for the expansion of the Territorial Army.

Top right: The first week in February 1942 was nominated as 'Warship Week' in Durham. This was one of the regular fund raising drives organised during the war to raise money for the struggle against fascism. Rather than just making an appeal for cash, the government used the idea that had been successful in World War I whereby money could be seen being directed towards a specific cause. Whether this really did happen is open to debate, but people believed that their pennies were helping to build a named destroyer and so opened their wallets more readily. In this case, Durham was set a target of £210,000, a huge sum over 60 years ago. Achievement of this figure meant that it could 'adopt' HMS Witherington, a short range destroyer that helped to successfully depth charge several U-boats operating in Atlantic and Mediterranean waters. During Warship Week, members of the armed forces paraded through the streets to publicise the event. This one began in Waddington Street and travelled through Market Place, where Lord Londonderry, the county's Lord Lieutenant, took the salute, before ending in Old Elvet. This photograph illustrates part of the role played by women in the military during the war. Those electing for the army joined the Auxiliary Territorial Service, budding aviators the Women's Auxiliary Air Force and mariners the Women's Royal Naval Service.

Above right: Bernard Law Montgomery (1887-1976) was only the 16th person to be granted the honour of becoming a Freeman of the City. This accolade was given to him in

January 1953 as a mark of respect for the man who had inspired our troops during World War II with his leadership qualities. Having graduated from Sandhurst, he fought with distinction during World War I and remained in the army, acquiring a reputation as an efficient and tough leader. In 1940, after the evacuation at Dunkirk, Montgomery commanded the southeastern section of England in anticipation of a German invasion. In August 1942 he was appointed as the commander of the 8th Army in North Africa and helped restore the morale of troops on the run from Rommel's German forces. His stunning victory at El Alamein in November 1942 was one of the turning points of the war and the church bells in Britain were rung for the first time since hostilities began. Under the command of the American General Eisenhower, with whom he had a frosty relationship, Montgomery led the Allied invasion of Normandy on D-Day in 1944. He was made a viscount in 1946 and went on to become deputy commander of NATO in the 1950s. He was warmly greeted in Market Place when he came to Durham and received a surprise gift from a police officer, William Plunkett, of a photograph of his brother, Canon Colin Montgomery, taken when a student at St Chad's College in 1926. 'Monty' went from Market Place to Palace Green, where he inspected a gathering of Durham Light Infantry cadets.

Soldiers have to go whenever and wherever duty calls. The cobblestones rang out to the sound of marching feet as the troops moved out, yet again. Large crowds of wellwishers gathered in Market Place to say their farewells on 20 July 1952 as members of the 1st Battalion Durham Light Infantry (DLI) made their way to the cathedral for a service of remembrance dedicated to the memory of the 3,000 who did not make it back after World War II. The forces were off to Korea, taking part in a war that meant little to us and being fought on a part of the globe few of us knew anything about and cared even less. As with participation in most conflicts, decisions were made in ivory towers in Whitehall and ordinary people went off into the unknown from where some would never return. The DLI story began in 1758 when General John Lambton first raised the 68th Regiment of Foot as part of the British Army. It later fought under Wellington and also saw active duty in the Crimean War. In 1881 it was transformed into the 1st Battalion of the DLI, with the 106th Regiment becoming the 2nd Battalion. After service in the Boer War, the DLI fought bravely in the trenches during World War I, when six of its men won Victoria Crosses. Further honours were won in the 1939-45 war and, when the DLI sailed off to Korea as part of the United Nations' troops, many of its young men were there on National Service and found themselves fighting in trench conditions similar to those experienced in the Great War. The Durhams lowered their colours in the cathedral on 12 December 1968 when they were subsumed into one large regiment, the Light Infantry.

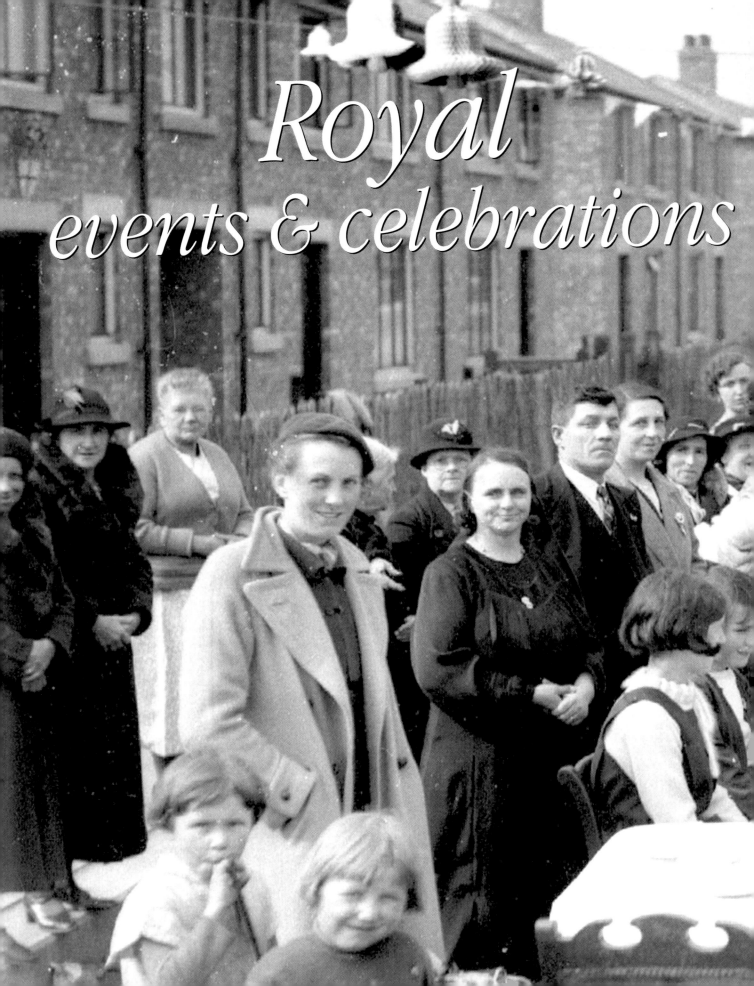

Royal
events & celebrations

Sherburn means bright or shiny stream and it was here that a village grew in the 19th century from the need to provide housing for miners and their families. Known locally as 'The Hill', the district thrived until the closure of the mine in 1965. The settlement lies to the east of Durham and is reached via the A181 that runs through Gilesgate. It was off this stretch of Sherburn Road that residents threw a street party to celebrate the coronation of King George VI in May 1937. Trestle tables were commandeered, cloths thrown across them and mums slaved away making cakes, sandwiches and jellies from specially shaped moulds that resembled rabbits or squirrels. The children loved them and washed down the goodies with lashings of fizzy pop as they feasted under the jolly bunting dancing above their heads. Little did the youngsters know, but King George VI was crowned on 12 May 1937 on the very day originally set aside for his brother, Edward VIII. He had abdicated in late 1936 when his affair with the American socialite, Wallis Simpson, split the nation into two camps. One side felt that he should follow his heart while the other demanded that he did his duty and put the monarchy and its stability to the forefront. George, or Albert as he really was, had to pick up the pieces, not easy for such a shy, diffident man. Britain rallied behind him and street parties such as this one went on long after the little ones were tucked up for the night.

Right: During the 1930s great strides were made in Durham to rid the city of the slums at Millburngate, Old Elvet and Framwellgate. Residents were rehoused on new council estates, one of the largest being built in the Sherburn Road area. Families were thrilled to have homes that were bright and clean. Inside toilets meant that the trip across the back yard tom the outdoor lavvy was a thing of the past. There was no longer a need to whistle when in there, with one foot carefully propping the door shut. Gone, too, was the old tin bath that was dragged inside and into the kitchen where it was filled from kettles boiled on the cooking range. The last in the family to get in always got the muckiest water, but now everyone could have a fresh dip as there was hot water literally on tap. This new development provided homes for 3,600 who had endured years of damp, unhealthy and dirty living conditions in dilapidated houses that, in some cases, were little more than hovels. Mr and Mrs Thomas Albrighton of 22 Fir Avenue were especially pleased with their new abode and were more than happy to tell their royal visitors all about it. King George VI and Queen Elizabeth stopped off during their tour of Durham on 23 February 1939 and received a warm greeting from all the residents. Unfortunately, time has not been kind and parts of the estate are now a little seedy in appearance.

Bottom left: Before the days of designer labels, shell suits and decidedly casual wear, men's tailoring was an important part of the face of every high street in the land. The Fifty Bob Tailor, Dunn's, Weaver to Wearer and Hepworth's all traded successfully, ensuring that Britain's males were neatly and economically turned out in suits and sports jackets. Some firms had their own catchy slogans that older readers remember today. Montague Burton was 'the tailor of taste' and John Collier had 'the window to watch'. During the late 1950s and 1960s, when television advertising really took off, men's clothing was a major player. There was one memorable advert showing shirts dancing on a washing line, promoting Rael-Brook poplin, 'the shirt you don't iron'. That was a quarter of a century after this photograph and it was not some animation that had brought thousands into Market Place on 23 February 1939. Nor was it the chance of getting a bargain at Hepworth's, but the more inspirational chance of getting a glimpse of their beloved King and Queen. There was not a single cobblestone left

uncovered as a seething mass of humanity squashed together to cheer the limousines as they pulled up outside the Guildhall. It was reported that there were some 3,000 schoolchildren in attendance who gave a lusty rendition of the national anthem.

Below: Who cared if the wind blew chilly and the frost sparkled on the ground? February 1939 was a cold month, but this day was brightened up by the royal visit. Nothing was going to stop this loyal group of subjects from literally waving the flag. Wrapped up warm, they waited patiently for the royal motorcade to pass by, clutching banners and Union flags that the thrifty amongst them had saved from the coronation less than two years before. Perhaps a couple of our more mature readers, now in their early 70s, can spot themselves on the front row and recall the thrill of seeing their King and Queen in the flesh. It was a momentous occasion, not really appreciated by modern society as it has become used to images being flashed across the world via satellite and television links. That makes us rather blasé about such events as we feel that we have a regular diet of matters to do with the monarchy. However, this group only caught glimpses of the monarchy via the occasional cinema newsreel or newspaper photograph, so when the chance came along to see royalty at first hand it was seized quickly. They did not know when the opportunity would present itself again. Schools closed, offices ceased to operate and factories ground to a halt as young and old found vantage points from where they could display their support. The little girl in the centre only got a brief glimpse as they passed by, but she knew that Queen Elizabeth's wave was meant just for her.

Above: The Girl Guides and Sea Rangers raised their standards on Palace Green. This was once the site of the old market place and, in early medieval times, was cluttered with wooden houses that were squashed together in a tight knit and rather insanitary community. Bishop Flambard cleared them away in the 12th century because of the danger to the cathedral from what he described as 'fire and filth'. It was from the buildings now around Palace Green that the Prince Bishops performed their administrative duties. In May 1951, in the shadow of the castle, HRH Princess Margaret Rose (1930-2002), sister to Queen Elizabeth II, was still to reach her majority, but was already the Commodore of the Sea Rangers. This branch of the Girl Guides was for older girls and originated as the Sea Guides before adopting its new name in 1920. Youngsters in the Guiding movement, even in the early days, dedicated themselves to a mixture of recreational and instructional activities. Robert Baden-Powell's sister, Agnes, and his wife, Olave, were the prime movers in generating the interest that led to its international appeal. Women, long past their active guiding years who may now be members of the Trefoil Guild, have been known to display the insignia patented in 1914 well into old age. Princess Margaret was a troubled soul who never found true happiness, being denied marriage to the divorced Peter Townsend in the 1950s, and only enjoying a short spell of joy with the husband she later divorced, Anthony Armstrong-Jones.

Below: The swinging 60s brought us the mini skirt, kinky boots, free love, pop groups, flower power and everything else we now associate with the rise in power of the youth culture. Yet, there were some old values that we clung to and cared little if they were regarded as the prerogative of the fuddy-duddy. Our lovely Queen, and the monarchy she represented, continued to attract large crowds of faithful subjects whenever she appeared in public. It had to be something special to make us turn out in the chill of the first days of spring, standing patiently in rows six deep, and she was just that. On 23 March 1967, Queen Elizabeth II, with Dean Wild walking a respectful pace behind her, visited our city and children grabbed little Union flags and waved them as she strolled past. Older members of the crowd remarked on her elegance and called out 'Good on you, ma'am,' as she performed her walkabout. Her Majesty had been attending a private sherry party for residents of the College and was on her way to join the Bishop and some 100 guests for lunch in the great hall of the castle. Earlier, the Queen had attended a service in the cathedral. Here she distributed Maundy money to a representative gathering. This tradition, in Britain originally a form of alms giving to the needy, developed from the European custom of the sovereign washing the feet of the poor on Holy Thursday, the day before Good Friday. This was the only time that the ceremony had taken place in Durham.

The signs for Gold Flake and Craven 'A' cigarettes, the ones you smoked 'for your throat's sake' according to adverts, looked rather incongruous when set alongside the Union flags and banners that bedecked the Town Hall. Built as the Guildhall in 1356, most of it was rebuilt in 1665. This was where guilds in the late Middle Ages met to confer about standards of work and to approve apprenticeships and qualifications as journeymen. The guilds were association of craftsmen or merchants, formed for mutual aid and protection and for the furtherance of their professional interests. On 17 May 1958 members of the Durham Light Infantry obeyed the command 'eyes left' as they marched across the setts on Market Place as part of the regiment's bicentenary celebrations. Princess Alexandra paid her first visit since being appointed Colonel in Chief by her cousin, Queen Elizabeth II. It was a considerable honour for a young woman in her 22nd year, but she carried off her duties from the specially erected dais with the elegance and serenity we expected from a member of the royal family. Princess Alexandra is the daughter of George, Duke of Kent and Princess Marina of Greece. In her teens, Princess Alexandra made sure that she would have a wider knowledge of the world than some of her peers had. On completing her education she took a nursing course at Great Ormond Street Hospital before starting to undertake official engagements. Her marriage to Angus Ogilvy in 1963 was one of the society events of that year.

Sporting life

Below: We know that the north is not all whippets and pigeon fancying, but such pastimes have provided pleasure for many a year. In this scene, John Pilkington, a resident of Gilesgate, showed his obvious pride as he carefully handled the bird that had won the Deerness Valley Federation race from Brussels in June 1949. The humble pigeon has been a friend of man since the pharaohs were lads. The earliest record of the domestication of pigeons is from the fifth Egyptian dynasty in about 3000 BC. The sultan of Baghdad established a pigeon post system in 1150 AD and Genghis Khan used such a method of transmitting news and information as his conquests spread. These birds were widely used for messenger service in Europe during the first part of the 19th century and pigeon racing became a popular sport in Belgium at this time. By the 1880s nearly every village had a Société Colombophile, translating loosely as 'pigeon-fanciers club'. Around this time, its popularity was becoming well established in this country. There are strict controls governing pigeon races and a bird is not considered to have arrived home until actually through the trap of its loft. During World War II these birds were used to carry messages to and from secret agents in occupied Europe. There were more instances of the Dickin Medal, the award for animal bravery, being given to pigeons than to any other creature.

Above: After the last war the public's appetite for spectator sport knew few bounds. Soccer stadiums were packed, cricket grounds put up 'house full' notices and lesser attractions like speedway saw the turnstiles clicking merrily. The upsurge in interest was not confined to the major venues. Even the smaller teams and clubs benefited from the desire to stand on the terraces and indulge in supporting the local side. Devotion to sides playing our national game was based on geography, not success. If you were born in Crewe, then that was the team for you, not some fancy Dan outfit from a big city, just because it had the star players. Durham folk cheered on their home team rather than making the traitorous journey to Roker Park or St James' Park. The match in progress here featured City against Sunderland 'A' team at Ferens Park in 1951 and was the first game to be played at this venue. It was the fourth ground used by the club since its formation after World War I, when it played in the Victory League. Durham City's first games were played at Garden House Park, where County Hall now stands. After one season it moved to Kieper Haughs before relocating to Holiday Park, named after a former mayor, in the mid 1920s. The club disbanded in 1938 and was not reformed until 1950. Ferens Park was sold in 1994 and, the following year, the club moved to New Ferens Park, now the Archibald's Stadium, at Belmont.

Alderman HC Ferens served as the soccer club's president for many years up to his death in 1978. He contributed out of his own pocket towards the purchase of the ground that was named after him and where Durham City played one of its most memorable games. Ferens Park was one of the best appointed venues in the northern League, boasting fine facilities that included a pleasant clubhouse, covered stand and floodlighting. It was also a picturesque spot to play in, though those on the field had little time to contemplate the rural setting on 7 November 1957. The attendance record of 7,000 was set in this second round match of the FA Cup when Wirral's Tranmere Rovers provided the opposition. Victory meant the chance to go into the hat with the big boys from the top two divisions of the Football League who joined the competition in round three. Players and spectators could

dream of getting a tie against cup holders Aston Villa or the Busby Babes from Manchester United. Home illusions were shattered when the visitors came out the victors by 3-0. At least that was an improvement on the last time the clubs met as Tranmere won that match in the late 1920s by an embarrassing 11-1. This was at the end of Durham's only period in major league football. It joined Division Three (North) in 1921, but failed to gain re-election at the end of the 1927-28 season. Two of the club's most successful players came from that era. George Camsell lived in Framwellgate Moor and impressed scouts from top clubs with his ability. In 1923 he was transferred to Middlesbrough for whom he scored an amazing 344 goals in a 16 year career at Ayresome Park. He also represented the national team, as did Sammy Crooks who moved on to Derby County in 1927 and won 26 caps for England.

Bird's eye view

Below: This serene view across Durham from the early 1930s shows how little change there has been to the main fabric of the place we have grown to love and admire. Little wonder that it has become a centre for pilgrims both religious and touristic, because its breathtaking beauty is a joy to behold. The buses and train at the railway station in the foreground may not be the most magnificent, but who can deny the splendour of the castle and cathedral that dominate the scene. The Cathedral Church of Christ and Blessed Mary Virgin, to give it its full name, is recognised by most as being the finest Norman cathedral in all Europe. It took 40 years to build and was commenced during the reign of William II, continued through most of Henry I's time on the throne and completed in 1133. The cathedral contains the relics of St Cuthbert and the Venerable Bede, notable religious figures in the northeast in Saxon times. The building is 470 feet in length and rises 218 feet above the heads of the congregation. The site of the castle has links with the Saxon era, when earth and wooden fortifications were built here, and was the scene for one major battle with William the Conqueror's force when all but one of 700 Normans were killed. After the King had retaliated with a harsh pogrom of measures that brought starvation to the local population, the Normans gained control and built their castle.

Above: Clickety-click, clickety-clack, oh how the sound of the wheels travelling over the gaps in the rails and across the points as steam gushes from the locomotive funnel reminds us of the halcyon days of rail travel. This photograph can be dated as a couple of years pre BC, namely Beeching cuts. He was the man entrusted by the government to take charge of British Railways in the early 1960s and who led the decimation of branch lines and stations that made him such a maligned figure. Looking at the steam train hurtling across the viaduct makes every anorak long for the days of the Mallard, the Flying Scotsman and the Silver Jubilee express locomotives of the golden age in the 1930s when speed records were smashed time after time. 'Faster than fairies, faster than witches', as RL Stevenson put it in his poem 'From a railway carriage'. They even inspired Vivian Ellis to compose 'Coronation Scot' in 1948, the catchy light classic that was used as the theme tune for the radio detective series, 'Paul Temple'. The viaduct carrying the railway into Durham station was built in 1857 by the Durham and Sunderland Railway Company. This was not the city's first station as there was an earlier one that opened in nearby Shincliffe in 1839. It was in use until 1893 when Elvet station began operations at the head of Old Elvet, where the magistrates' courts were built in 1963, though the station had been closed since 1931.

The first Framwellgate Bridge was built in around 1120 by order of Bishop Flambard and it was there that Ralph Neville murdered his cousin Richard Fitzmarmaduke in 1318, following a longstanding family feud between these two rich and influential men. The old borough, which the bridge linked to Silver Street, took its name from the description of its whereabouts as the path (gate) from the well, the main source of the city's water in the Middle Ages. Bishop Langley, supported by cathedral funding, replaced this bridge some 300 years later. The gatehouse at the eastern end was taken down in 1760 and the bridge widened in 1856. It was the first major bridge to be built across the Wear and, until the construction of Millburngate Bridge, carried all the traffic from the west coming into Durham. Younger readers must shudder at the picture they can conjure up of the chaos here as cars, lorries and buses attempted to get across from one side of the city to another, jammed bumper to bumper and side to side as they made their way along narrow Silver Street. In July 1952, it was not traffic that streamed across the bridge, but people on the march, making their way to the miners' gala. The view across the Wear also takes in the viaduct, towards the top left of the picture, with just six of its eleven 100 foot arches visible.

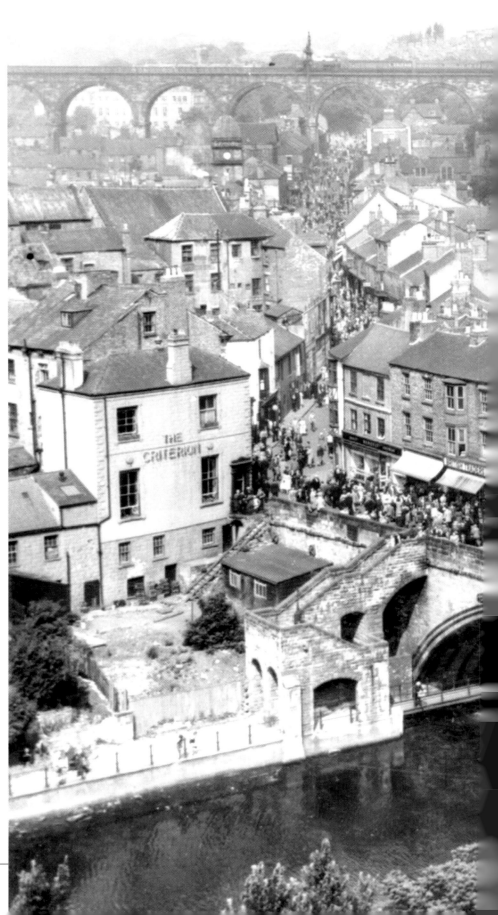

Working life

Above: It was largely a female staff in the finishing room at Durham Carpets, as seen on 28 September 1954, where goods were prepared prior to dispatch. Until the 19th century, rugs and carpets were handmade and were often of such high artistic quality that they were usually considered works of art. Their design and execution reached its highest artistic quality in Persia in the 15th and 16th centuries. Mechanisation transformed carpet making in the 19th and 20th centuries. The power loom made its appearance in 1839 and further significant strides were made in the 1920s, when the high speed tufting process was introduced where a pre-woven backing fabric moves through a high-speed machine as a bank of giant needles inserts individual tufts into the material. Durham Carpets produced goods that were practical but also retained some of the aesthetic quality of those crafted in earlier times. Hugh Mackay (1849-1924) established his own factory after Crossley's took over Gilbert Henderson's, throwing him out of work. After his death, his son Lawrence expanded the business and, by 1929, was demonstrating his wares at the North East Coastal Exhibition. With a nice eye for a touch of humour, one of Lawrence's most successful products was the Yakcam carpet, which is the family name spelt backwards! The factory site was where Millennium Place now stands, off Claypath. Arsonists damaged it in 1969 and the company moved to Dragonville in 1980.

Below The first supermarkets in Britain were not like the mammoth shopping malls we know today. Now that Asda has even overtaken Marks and Spencer as the leading clothing retailer on the high street, it seems likely in the future that such stores will move further and further away from their initial foray into self service food sales. Perhaps in a few years' time we will do our banking, buy all our white goods and even get our new motorcars from a supermarket department. In 1958, when this store embraced the shopping revolution inherited from across the Atlantic, serving yourself and making your way to the cash till having done the shopping under one roof was an attractive novelty. Little did these housewives appreciate that they were sounding the death knell for many established individual shopkeepers. They could not compete with the cost cutting exercises of the larger establishments that bought cheaply in bulk, had lower pro rata overheads and were able to pass on these savings to their customers. Some indulged in cynical loss leader practices, accepting short term negative returns in the sure knowledge that smaller competitors would be driven to the wall. Some of the original supermarkets were really glorified grocers but, before too long, the big boys had made their mark and created something of a monopoly for themselves.

Below: There is something truly satisfying about working with your hands to create something. It may only be a small pot thrown on a wheel, a sweater knitted for a loved one or a wooden toy whittled for a grandchild, but there is a real feeling of achievement on completion. Master craftsmen have that same emotion of job satisfaction when they complete their tasks, but their work is on a grander and more skilful scale. Here we have three such practitioners, all adept at their trade. They were employed in the ancient workshops at Durham Cathedral on 31 January 1936, where they took a pride in their work as only such artists in wood can do. Walter Hollis (centre) and Mr WS Cope (right) were accompanied by Thomas Jopling who was standing on the left by the magnificently carved door at the northern entrance to St Cuthbert's Shrine that, two days earlier, had been dedicated to the memory of his grandfather, the late WH Jopling. Referred to by the Dean as 'a fine old English craftsman', Mr Jopling began work on the carving on the door shortly before his death. Mr Hollis completed it to the same standard of artistic craftsmanship that his mentor displayed. Thomas Jopling continued the family tradition of gifted woodworkers and, at the time of this photograph, was studying at Sunderland Technical College.

Above: Lillian Crampton's shop in New Elvet was doing good business on 17 July 1954. She can be seen standing behind the outdoor stall next to her son, David, who later took over the business and continued to trade here until his retirement. By the time that this scene was photographed, rationing had just come to an end. It is amazing that it lasted so long. Brought in as a wartime measure, it went on for half as long again as the duration of hostilities with the enemy. By this date, of course, many items had been off the ration list for some time. But officially, housewives still needed coupons to buy meat until 3 July of this year. They could not even get a decent supply of rabbit meat as myxomatosis decimated the bunny population. For the first time since late 1939, London's Smithfield Market opened at midnight instead of 6 am. However, just as spivs saw a quick profit from the black market during the 1940s, so some butchers took advantage and immediately raised their prices. Members of the National Federation of Housewives dug out their notebooks and scoured the shops checking charges. Their chairman said that protest meetings would be held if costs did not come down. Ceremonial ration book burning took place at several Conservative Association meetings as the last direct link with wartime austerity came to its belated conclusion.

Above: In early 1960, Joe Sanders was working hard at the loom that was making a carpet for a very special occasion. Princess Margaret Rose, the Queen's sister, was to be married on 6 May to Anthony Armstrong-Jones, a fashion photographer. She drove from Buckingham Palace to Westminster Abbey for the ceremony that celebrated the first major royal wedding since Princess Elizabeth married Prince Philip in 1947. Large crowds cheered the happy couple who received many gifts from private individuals and businesses, in addition to those from family and friends. A smiling Joe helped provide a uniquely designed memento from Durham Carpets, the firm established by Hugh Mackay in September 1903 when he leased machinery and buildings from Henderson's carpet factory. Hugh was 54 at the time and had been a Henderson employee for 42 years, having started there at the tender age of just 12. He could certainly claim to know his stuff after such a long apprenticeship! Hugh ran his company until his death in 1924 and the business continued in his family's hands almost up to the end of the last century. Princess Margaret would have been pleased with the quality of her carpet as the Mackays had a fine reputation in the trade. The gift will definitely have outlasted the marriage as the couple divorced in 1978.

Top right: Saddler Street was part of the medieval route from Market Place to the cathedral. At that time it was known as Saddlergate, which is virtually the same as its current designation because 'gate' is an old word for 'road'. It does not take too much brainpower to determine the main commercial activity that must once have been centred here. The lower part of Saddler Street was once referred to as Fleshergate, from the practice of butchers slaughtering cattle in the street.

Durham mustard was produced near here in the 18th century from a factory on the western side of the street. A certain Mrs Clements originated a special way of extracting a pungent flavour from mustard seed by grinding it as if producing flour. In later years the secrets and the business passed into the hands of Colman's of Norwich. Whether or not these workmen undertaking road repairs on 7 October 1960 were as keen as mustard has not been recorded, but they seem to be bending their backs. The sounds of Roy Orbison's 'Only the lonely', new in the pop charts that week, might have drifted towards them through an open window next to a radio. They would not have heard Ricky Valance's 'Tell Laura I love her' as the BBC had banned it because of the morbid theme of the death of a racing driver. Thanks to airtime on Radio Luxembourg, though, it topped the hit parade.

Right: Clover Cottage and Williamson's shop on the corner of Crossgate Peth were demolished in 1966. This was the year that our national soccer team won its only major soccer trophy when Bobby Moore lifted the Jules Rimet World Cup at Wembley and everyone praised the eyesight of a Russian linesman; everyone outside West Germany, that is. It was also the time when television advertising was becoming established as the major source of attracting custom. By now, nearly every

household had a goggle box in the corner of the living room and manufacturers thought up new ideas for promoting their wares. They used humour, catchy jingles and freebies to catch our attention and get us to use their products in preference to others. Memorable slogans that easily identified a company or its goods were high on the list of ideas these companies went for. They employed writers to come up with a few words that were worth their weight in gold. Petrol companies introduced us to 'keep going well, keep going Shell' and Esso's 'tiger in the tank', but television gave a new lease of life to some that were already established. Motor racing's Murray Walker came up with 'a Mars a day helps you work, rest and play', not long after the war when he was a young advertising executive, and it more than stood the test of time. The 'drinka pinta milka day' slogan, seen on the left, first came to life in 1959, but was still on billboards and television screens many years later.

Adding sparkle to our lives

They say that diamonds are a girl's best friend. But of course its not just diamonds that girls find attractive, there are many kinds of precious stones and precious metals. For all of recorded history both men and women have been fascinated with the eternal flawless beauty of jewellery made from gold and silver, pearls, rubies and sapphires. Inevitably there grew up a cadre of skilled craftsmen who could enhance the intrinsic beauty of the materials they worked with. As an important centre in ages past Durham was no stranger to goldsmiths, silversmiths and jewellers. Today that long local tradition is continued by Bramwells, the well known local family firm of jewellers from which generations of local folk have bought not only jewellery but also those most personal and treasured items, wedding and engagement rings.

The Bramwells story can be traced back to the 19th century. In 1867 the young Elliott Bramwell moved from Garrigill near Aiston to Darlington and opened his own watchmakers and jewellers shop. There he married Sarah Jane Harbron and took her brother Charlie into partnership, to trade as Bramwell & Harbron.

One of Elliott and Sarah's sons, Harry, would stay in Darlington to work in his father's business. The eldest son William Arthur Bramwell however would go to Dublin to train before moving to Durham. There William gradually bought a watchmaker, jeweller and silversmith business at 24 Elvet Bridge from the widow of a Mr Brewster. He was accepted as a member of the National Association of Goldsmiths and Opticians in 1912.

Before the depression of the 1930s there would be about five men in the workshop at Elvet Bridge repairing watches, clocks and jewellery, as well as a couple of assistants in the

Top: *William Arthur Bramwell.*
Right: *William Arthur Bramwell's certificate of membership of the National Association of Goldsmiths, Jewellers, Silversmiths & Opticians.*

shop. Arthur was a skilled craftsman and produced beautiful hand-made replicas of Saint Cuthbert's pectoral Cross, one of which would be presented to the Queen when she visited Durham during her coronation year. The firm still specialises in Saint Cuthbert's Cross replicas in various sizes and forms, many of which have found their way to far flung parts of the world.

Arthur was also an accomplished photographer and his work features in a number of publications. He was a founder member of Durham Photographic Society and the Pen and Camera Club of Methodism

Never resting on his laurels Arthur studied optics by correspondence course, and began to test eyes in a room above the jewellers shop. As the optical practice expanded Arthur's younger brother Louis Clifford Bramwell who had trained with an optician in Coventry was brought in. As a result the opticians separated off, transferring next door to 26 Elvet Bridge, on the corner next to the Magdalene steps, before eventually moving to the present site next to the bridge, previously owned by hat makers Edith and Annie Catherall.

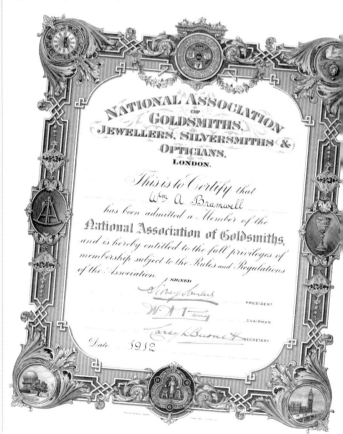

youngest son Clifford, entered the business in 1968. Peter trained in the workshop under Fred, and would accompany him up the tower to the Cathedral clock at dead of night to change the hour when British Summer Time began and ended.

Fred Wharton also looked after the municipal clocks in St Nicholas' church in the Market Place, and in the tower of the Essoldo Cinema in North Road. He was responsible for winding them every week, something he did for many years, until electric winding mechanisms were fitted.

The optical practice was continued by Arthur's second son (also called William Arthur), and later by his son, Christopher.

Meanwhile Arthur's daughter Winifred joined her father in the jewellers after leaving school and before joining the army during the war.

Business during the war years was very difficult. New jewellery was very scarce, and although some could be had on the 'Black Market'. Arthur however refused to trade in this way, and managed to scrape by on repairs. Business though was hardly encouraged just after the war when purchase tax on luxuries peaked at 125%.

Arthur died in the mid 1950s; as he had grown older the upper room at the shop had become a meeting place where he would discuss philosophy with a circle of learned friends from the clergy and the university whilst Winifred, who had gained her Jewellers Diploma in 1949, ran the shop.

Business slowly recovered after the war. Winifred ran the business with one shop assistant, and John Nelson in the workshop. Like Arthur, John Nelson too was getting on in years but had worked at Bramwells since he was apprenticed there when he left school. He was a familiar character in the town, and easily recognisable as he had a stiff leg.

After John Nelson retired Fred Wharton was employed as watch and clock repairer. Peter Bramwell, the son of Arthur's

Top and centre: *The Queen is presented with the beautiful hand-made replica of Saint Cuthbert's pectoral Cross (pictured centre) made by William Arthur Bramwell.*
Right: *Winifred Bramwell.*

Peter Bramwell qualified in gemmology, studied diamond grading at the London Gem Testing Laboratories, and became a National Association of Goldsmiths Registered Valuer. He was president of Durham City & District Chamber of Trade for many years.

In 1974 the rather shabby and not very secure Victorian shop front was replaced with a new, modern facade, and the interior restyled. This happened just at the time when Elvet Bridge became a pedestrian area. Although some other surrounding shopkeepers complained of lack of business, the new arrangements suited Bramwells, and the newly styled shop was a great success with customers. Five years later the opportunity came along to extend the workshops and offices above the adjacent properties to provide the extra capacity the growing business needed.

Most of the stock for the shop had always been bought through wholesalers, but in the late 1970s Peter Bramwell got together with a few like-minded jewellers in other parts of the country to found The Company of Master Jewellers. This is a co-operative buying and marketing group that enables its members to be more

competitive by pooling their buying power. The group is able to buy direct from manufacturing sources in the UK, Europe and other parts of the world, and this has made an important contribution to the success of the business.

1981 saw a return to Darlington, with the acquisition of Bartlett's Jewellers following the retirement of the owners. Raymond Wood, who continued to work for Bramwells until he was 80, was given the job of managing the shop.

Winifred died in 1982, at the age of 69; she had continued to work full-time until then. Going to bed feeling a bit tired after a long day at a trade fair, Winifred was unable to get up the next day, and was found to have a broken pelvis, which never healed.

William John Bramwell, the son of Arthur's eldest son Ernest, had joined the firm in 1975; he become a partner in 1981.

In 1988 William, also a qualified gemmologist, moved to Darlington where he and his wife Jill have moved the business to a larger shop in Post House Wynd, and opened The Silver Shop next door.

has become one of the North East's major wedding-ring stores. Bramwells aims to be the destination of choice for anyone wanting to buy good jewellery and watches in the North East of England.

Since the new shop lacked workshop and office space, Bramwells has retained the old shop on Elvet Bridge which now concentrates on more traditional, antique and second-hand jewellery, as well as pawnbroking, and carrying out the office functions for all of the four shops.

Today some 30 people work in the business, including Peter's son Tony, the fifth generation of the Bramwell family, who joined the firm after university. Tony holds the Retail Jewellers Diploma and has studied diamond grading with the Antwerp Diamond High Council.

Bramwells prides itself in being able to offer all the services one would expect from a quality jeweller. Nowadays when the majority of jewellers shops are simply showrooms with no workshop capability, Bramwells still maintains its own well-equipped workshops - and with experience going back five generations it can tackle almost any job. The business can even make items that would be otherwise difficult to obtain, and has carried out commissions for organisations all over the world.

When it comes to jewellery it's surely Bramwells not diamonds which are a girl's best friend!

Meanwhile back in Durham by 2001 Bramwells was bursting out of the little shop on Elvet Bridge and in December that year opened a large new showroom on the corner of Saddler Street and the Prince Bishop Shopping Centre. The new shop had a more contemporary style, concentrating on Designer Collections; it

Top left: *A view inside Bramwells circa 1960.*
Top right: *Early 1970s and Fred Wharton closes up for the day.* **Right:** *Peter and Tony Bramwell pictured outside Bramwells Elvet Bridge premises.*

A reflection on water

The roots of Northumbrian Water Limited are firmly based in the northeast, with its head office being located at Pity Me, on the outskirts of Durham City.

Serving more than 2.6 million customers in an area stretching from the Scottish borders to North Yorkshire, not only is Northumbrian Water one of the largest employers in the Durham area, it is also the largest environmental company in the northeast of England, committed to creating a cleaner, safer and healthier environment for future generations. A further 1.7 million customers in the southeast also benefit from the experience of Northumbrian Water (under the brand name of Essex & Suffolk Water).

The company that we know today has a long and varied history, its northern assets include reservoirs - high up in the Northumbrian hills and down deep in the Tees Valley. There is one name that is synonymous with the Durham area'swater supply and the 1950s local politics - that of Peter Lee.

Clean water crusader Peter Lee was instrumental in the construction of the Burnhope reservoir at Wearhead. But whilst his name was given to Peterlee on the East Durham coast (one of the 1950s post-war new towns),

the story of water supply to this area goes much further back in history.

In the second half of the 19th century there were several developments in the supply of water to Durham and surrounding areas. In 1860, a group of local gentlemen formed the Consett Waterworks Company, mainly to supply the three ironworks in the Consett district and the local population of approximately 20,000. Whilst initially most of the water needed was obtained from springs on Muggleswick Moor and from open catchwaters, by 1872 the Smiddy Shaw reservoir had been completed; Hisehope reservoir following in 1906.

In 1865 a second company was using the great water resources of the moors, with the Waskerley and Tunstall reservoirs being constructed in 1879-80. By 1902 these two smaller companies had amalgamated to become the Weardale and Consett Water Company and by 1914 were supplying an area of approximately 412 square miles, including 111 parishes, 22 rural and urban councils, and most significantly, the City of Durham.

In the run up to 1919, there was an increase in the population and industry flourished in the area, both of

Top: *Durham County Water Board, circa 1920.*

which lead to greater demands on the company. By the end of the first world war, those responsible for the wellbeing of the county had decided that a public enterprise, rather than private company, was needed and in July 1919, the Durham County Water Board (DCWB) was formed. The DCWB was made up of representatives from the area's county, rural and urban councils, with Peter Lee as chairman. Many of the developments in water supply to the Durham area are still attributed to the vision, courage and foresight of Peter Lee.

The Sunderland and South Shields Water Company (S&SSWC) had come into being in 1852; it relied

Top: Dalton pumping station circa 1900s. **Below:** Peter Lee cutting the first sod for Burnhope reservoir. **Right:** A plaque in commemoration of Peter Lee.

mainly on underground supplies from the Permian series of limestones along the coastal areas of County Durham, and Tyne and Wear. Many ornate pumping stations were constructed during this time, the majority of which are still standing, although their vastness is no longer a true representation of the modern, and very much smaller, equipment that they now house. As this source of water became fully exploited, a joint venture between DCWB and S&SSWC resulted in the construction of the Burnhope reservoir (1930-1936) in Weardale.

The reservoir was jointly owned but managed by DCWB. However, the companies' roles were reversed in a second joint venture, when the Derwent reservoir, near Consett, which was jointly owned but constructed and managed by S&SSWC.

The current company was formed out of many mergers and changes in legislation. In 1974, the government formed ten regional water authorities in England and Wales, which meant that DCWB became part of the Northumbrian Water Authority (NWA).

IN COMMEMORATION OF
PETER LEE,
CHAIRMAN OF THE DURHAM COUNTY WATER BOARD
1920 TO 1935,
WHO BY HIS ABLE GUIDANCE
CONTRIBUTED IN NO SMALL MEASURE TO THE
SATISFACTORY CONSTRUCTION OF BURNHOPE RESERVOIR
THIS MEMORIAL IS THE WORKERS TRIBUTE
TO HIS GREAT ABILITY AND CONSTANT ENDEAVOUR
TO PROMOTE THEIR WELFARE.

The year 1989 saw the privatisation of the water industry. NWA changed its name to Northumbrian Water Group (NWG) and was

floated on the stock exchange. Around the same time, the giant French company Lyonnaise des Eaux (LdE) bought the S&SSWC and Newcastle and Gateshead Water Company (N&GWC), merging them in 1992 to form North East Water (NEW). It was in 1996 that LdE purchased the majority of shares in NWG and merged it with NEW, forming the new Northumbrian Water Group. However, life in the water industry is seldom static, and in 2003, SUEZ (as LdE was now called) announced that it was to sell 75% of its share holding, which resulted in the company being floated once again on the stock exchange.

The Northumbrian Water Group currently owns and operates 32 impounding (or catchment) reservoirs, 43 water treatment works and 268 service (or treated water storage) reservoirs. Water is supplied to customers using gravity in the first instance, along nearly 17,000km of water main, although it also has 250 pumping stations should gravity need a helping hand.

Top: *Burnhope reservoir's gauge house.*
Right: *An aerial view of Burnhope reservoir.*

The company's first water treatment works to be built for over a decade has recently been completed in the Wear Valley and treats the water from Peter Lee's Burnhope reservoir. Wear Valley water treatment works replaced the Wearhead and Tunstall water treatment works, both of which were coming to the end of their working lives. Costing in excess of £25 million, Wear Valley water treatment works has been designed to maintain the very high standard of drinking water currently enjoyed by some 200,000 customers in the County Durham area.

Wear Valley water treatment works has been designed to minimise its impact on, and to blend into, the landscape of the area of outstanding natural beauty that surrounds it. Looking to all purposes like an Upper Weardale farmstead, most of the works are buried into the hillside, with the external building being built of natural stone, slate and timber. Plans are in place to demolish the old Wearhead works, and in its place a wetland nature reserve will be created to encourage wildlife, especially the local population of endangered water voles. There will also be a pond-dipping area for educational visits.

However, Northumbrian Water does not only deal with clean water, it is also responsible for sewerage services to its 2.6 million customers in the northeast. Sewage (or wastewater as it is sometimes called) is collected through a series of more than 21,000km of sewers and taken to one of 426 sewage treatment works, assisted, where necessary, by more than 600 sewage pumping stations.

The Durham area is particularly well served with the Barkers Haugh sewage treatment works sitting on the banks of the River Wear in the midst of the city itself; other works are based in the surrounding areas. After intensive treatment, the treated water from the sewage is returned to the environment, whilst the sewage sludge is transported by road tanker and ship to the Regional Sludge Treatment Centre (RSTC) on Teesside, where it is dried into 'biopellets'. Those biopellets can be used in agriculture. Recently however the company has also signed a ground breaking deal with the Lafarge Cement UK's Cauldon Works in Staffordshire, which will use biopellets to replace some of the coal and petroleum coke traditionally used to fire its kilns. This is an environmental sound solution, which will see a useful product coming from waste.

So next time you turn your tap on, think of Peter Lee and his vision to bring clean water to the people of Durham - and raise your glass to him and the many who have followed in his footsteps.

Top: Wear Valley water treatment works.
Below: An aerial view of of Dawdon sewage treatment works.

Quality and innovation from Bowburn to Beijing

Process Scientific Innovations, or PSI as it was more generally known - and PSI Global Ltd (the company changed its name in 1999 to more accurately reflect its international standing) has been situated at Bowburn Industrial Estate South (on the site of the old Bowburn Colliery) since its beginnings. It has expanded from occupying just one unit to its current 20,000 sq ft. factory complex.

The business was created in 1976 to manufacture filters and separators for the compressed air and vacuum industries. The firm's founders were Sue and George Hunter who had recently left the now-competing firm of Domnick Hunter plc. As a result of some imaginative initial research by the pair, the Greek letter PSI Ψ, a clever play on words on pounds per square inch, was adopted as the company's logo. The new enterprise started with just four staff, including its two founders, but now employs over 100 local people.

Taking a big plunge, an innovative pleating machine was bought in Germany at a cost of £20,000. The idea behind pleated elements (designed to deliver a greater surface area to filter out more impurities) was patented, and the machine is still in operation today.

In the first year, turnover would be just £11,873. By the early years of the 21st century that turnover had soared to more than £5m.

The company's filtration and separation technology innovations have resulted in over a hundred patents in many countries all over the world for its ultra high-efficiency products. An on-going improvement programme aimed at solving industries' problems through Research and Development has enabled the company to leapfrog its competitors in terms of technical superiority.

The continuous improvement through research and development which resulted in the introduction of pleated

Above: *Founders Sue and George Hunter.*
Below: *Process Scientific Innovations' first exhibition stand, Switzerland, 1978.*

glass micro fibre elements in 1976 also led to the in-house manufacture of patented moulded media in 1978. From the early 1980s, PSI Global was the only filter manufacturer in the world to make a patented moulded filter tube using its own media. An international patent was placed on a new drainage layer in 1998. PSI Global now sells this and other filtration and separation technology to its marketplace competitors under license: ironically this includes Domnick Hunter plc, the company that the Hunters originally left.

Long term growth would be fuelled by exports. In the late 1970s early 1980s, PSI Global was exporting 99% of its products to Europe and, out of necessity, Sue Hunter took all her four children with her on trips to visit customers abroad. As UK credit cards were not widely accepted abroad (especially in Germany) at that time, Sue was forced to take all the appropriate currencies with her in various purses and money bags! In 1989, despite the weakness of the Pound Sterling against a basket of major currencies, the company was awarded The Queen's Award for Export.

The Hunter children also 'helped' with packing of products in the early years but this usually ended in general playtime around the despatch area. However, this early exposure to their parents' workplace got them used to the PSI Global plant and its products - something that would serve them well in later years.

Above: A view inside PSI Global's factory in the 1980s.
Right: Sue Hunter, 2004.

Sue Hunter remains as Managing Director (George retired from the business in 1995). Each of their four children have joined and left the family-run company at various times over the years. Jon Hunter joined the production department in 1982. He is now MD of a wholly-owned subsidiary company. Alex Hunter joined the R&D team in the technical department in 1990 and now runs IP02, a company supplying technical services to PSI Global Ltd. Daniel Hunter who joined the sales department in 1992 is now Commercial Director. Lastly David Hunter, who joined in 1996 as a production engineer, is now Operations Director. Each of the brothers has worked his way up from junior positions.

Today, 80 percent of the company's filters and separators for vacuum pumps and compressors are exported all over the world, to Europe, the USA and Canada, Australasia and the Far East.

For the future, PSI Global aims to maintain its Bowburn manufacturing base whilst continuing to develop globally with business partners in the USA and the Far East.

Plastic made perfect

Veriplast International, based on the Dragonville Industrial Estate, is one of Europe's leading vending cup manufacturers. But though disposable plastic cups and containers may be icons of the modern age the company has a heritage that goes back to the early 1900s.

The business was founded in 1907 by EZ Taylor, an American engineer who already had a company supplying industrial pails. Mono's offices were located within those of the Taylor Hygienic Pail Company in Clerkenwell London. The basis of the original Mono company was disposable paper milk pots.

In a fascinating aside EZ Taylor set sail in April 1912 aboard the ill-fated White Star Liner SS Titanic in the company of his wife, together with a co-director, Mr Williams. When the liner collided with the iceberg Taylor felt the impact, dressed and went on deck to investigate. A ship's officer told him to put on his life jacket and go at once to the boat deck. Taylor returned to his cabin and woke his wife before going to wake Williams. Williams however refused to join the Taylors on the boat deck, declaring that the ship was unsinkable. Mr and Mrs Taylor were amongst the first to leave the ship; Williams drowned alongside 1,500 other victims of the disaster.

That same year a new production unit was established at Park Royal, West London. With the outbreak of war in 1914 however, many of the male employees soon joined the armed services and the new factory took on many girls. At the same time the company opened a factory in France and another in the USA.

Top left: *Founder, EZ Taylor.* **Right and below:** *Early 20th century pictures of men in the Printing Department and girls in the Rolling Room.*

Following the war business picked up quickly. Production was focused on cream pots and containers for jam and marmalade. In 1922 the company decided to reduce all its prices by one third for the Dairy Show at the Royal Agricultural Hall. The result was a bumper crop of orders. Ten years later turnover was £235,000 and 104 million pots were being produced each year.

During the 1930s subsidiary companies would be opened in Dublin and in Cape Town, South Africa. The original Park Royal site was expanded to accommodate the increasing demand for pots to be used for ice cream.

The directors of Mono Containers anticipated the fall in business which the outbreak of the second world war in 1939 would bring and obtained Government contracts to make packing cases for ammunition and shells. These contracts enabled the company to survive the war with business levels virtually intact, despite the Park Royal factory being a repeated casualty of the war. In 1940 the factory suffered extensive damage when its roof was set on fire by a German bomb. In 1944 part of the factory was damaged by a VI flying bomb, and later in that same year more damage was sustained from two more flying bombs.

During the mid-1950s new materials came on the market and the company began to experiment with making cups from polystyrene. In 1957 it was a agreed that the company would focus product development on those new plastic cups.

The plastic cup production process demanded that the operation work a three shift pattern. Good labour was hard to come by in the south of England and as a consequence a decision was made to relocate to Durham where the company already had a small satellite factory making plastic trays. The Durham site was completely redeveloped and opened in 1960. Within three years all business had been transferred to Durham

At this time annual turnover was £1,214,000, of which only some £500,000 was in plastic: but plastics would soon come to dominate.

In the early 1960s Mono secured an exclusive agreement with Bellaplast Company of Wiesbaden, Germany to take a new type of plastic thermoform machine. At the time hot drinks vending machines were just beginning to take off in the UK and the demand for the new plastic cups grew in line with this, largely to satisfy new legal requirements for tea breaks.

After a number of approaches in the early 1970s Mono Containers Ltd was finally acquired by Autobar in 1977. Autobar had also acquired Fibracan in 1976, based in Skelmersdale. These two factories have an amazing annual output of no fewer than 3 billion cups, pots and containers which are often used in every day life - vending cups, water cups, yoghurt pots, cream pots, salad bowls, beer glasses and chinese takeaways....all now under the Veriplast International name.

Top left: *Employees and employee incentive strategies used in 1922.* ***Above:*** *Ice-cream pot used in the early 1950s.* ***Below:*** *Veriplast International's purpose built factory in Durham completed in 1998. Further developments on the site to be completed in 2004.*

On the house

with a special interest in Durham City, Geoffrey Wood was well known and respected throughout the area.

A further office was opened in Consett and in 1972 Mr Wood was joined by Keith Johnson, firstly as Assistant and then as a Partner. Following Geoffrey Wood's untimely death in 1974, Keith Johnson took over as Senior Partner. As a fairly young and inexperienced Chartered Surveyor, with a total staff of 6 and the reputation of J W Wood to uphold, the firm expanded rapidly with the addition of further offices throughout the County and a major move in the early 1980s to the present address at 7 Old Elvet.

Great changes have taken place in estate agency and surveying. When Keith Johnson started with the firm it had one old photocopier, less than 10% of the population of Durham had a telephone and communication was, in the main, by letter. By the late 1980s the firm had grown to 11 branches with 8 partners and 60 staff. Another great change took place when financial institutions started to buy up the main local practices. In 1987 the firm was sold to the General Accident Insurance

Top left: *Geoffrey Wood conducting an auction.*
Below: *Early JW Wood documents from the 1920s.*

J W Wood & Son was established in 1910 by Joseph Watson Wood based in premises in North Road, Durham. Joseph Wood's forte was as an auctioneer, conducting livestock sales and being part of the Durham & District Livestock Mart Limited.

The firm also ran a charabanc and taxi firm from the premises. Mr Wood also was deeply involved in the community, being elected Mayor of the old City of Durham in November 1931. The firm was later transferred to Mr Wood's son Geoffrey, who had served with the Durham Light Infantry during the War.

The firm subsequently moved to premises in Claypath which included the Oddfellows Hall, where regular furniture and antique auctions were held, in addition to expanding the estate agency business as more of the local population looked to buy their first home. A noted historian

residential sales side but in particular for the residential lettings and property management together with the creation of the new commercial department. Mayflower Mortgages, which was formed in conjunction with Steve Easter, adjoins the J W Wood office. Today 35 J W Wood staff enjoy excellent working conditions in the superb environment which has been created for clients.

Since 1910 there have been only 3 senior partners of Woods, the founder, J W Wood, his son Geoffrey Wood and now Keith Johnson. The firm is proud of its ongoing tradition to not only provide professional services to the locality but with its contribution to a number of charities, hopes to continue its involvement in the community.

Life has certainly changed since 1910, with every member of staff now having a computer terminal with an internal and external network, their own personal email and communication via mobile phone. All properties are now displayed on the Internet and yet, a great deal of what they do has not changed in the last 90 years - they still advertise in the Durham Advertiser, Northern Echo and Journal, as they did 90 years ago; they still interact with their clients on a one-to-one and personal basis and their philosophy is still about providing a quality service in a professional manner.

Group (as it then was) and Keith Johnson became the Regional Managing Director of the Group, responsible for County Durham, Northumberland and Cumbria.

The pendulum however swung again, and in 1992 Keith Johnson agreed to buy back the firm from the insurance group and J W Wood changed into its present form. With the original founder directors, Margaret Ashworth, Geoff Graham and John Burton, the new company has once again flourished, with seven offices throughout County Durham and Darlington providing a complete general practice relating to residential, commercial and all aspects of property transactions, valuation and surveying. The auction house has gone but Keith Johnson still keeps with the J W Wood tradition of auctioneering by conducting occasional property auctions and by being involved in charity auctions throughout the County.

The new millennium brought further changes. When the office first moved to Old Elvet there were 12 occupants, but the firm, with its various departments, now housed some 28 staff and accommodation capable of supporting only 15 desking-sharing had become a necessity. The problem was solved in 2002 with the rebuilding and extension of the premises to provide state of the art accommodation, not only for the

Top left: Celebrations as Keith Johnson agrees to buy back the firm, 1992. *Below:* JW Wood, 7 Old Elvet.

Part of the landscape

With almost 800 staff the Land Registry is one of Durham's largest employers. It was in 1965, more than a century after the first Land Registration Act, that a small group of Civil Servants opened the Registry's most northerly office.

The government's post-war plans were in fact to move the entire Land Registry to Durham from London, but in the end that honour was given to the Post Office Savings Certificate Division accommodated in the controversial Millburngate House on the riverside.

By comparison the Land Registry's growth was slow and unobtrusive. Its first home, the old County Court building, was one of several buildings in the Elvet Waterside area later demolished to make way for the new bridge.

Survivors of that first group recall it as a leisurely process. Those who passed a drawing test began exhaustive exercises in the linework, brushwork and lettering that then went into hand-drawn plans. Others struggled with the Legal Practice Book - two volumes

of near-biblical authority - and took up a pen to draft the register entries that recorded 'Property', 'Proprietor' and 'Mortgages'.

Facilities were basic: a kettle and handful of luncheon vouchers. The proximity of Brown's Boat Yard meant staff could go rowing at lunchtime. To anyone fresh from school it seemed rather like being a student.

Within a year, however, the growing operation moved to a new building leased from the County Council next to the new Police headquarters at Aykley Heads.

The large rooms came in handy when the Land Registry joined the Durham District Table Tennis League: with the desks moved aside there was plenty of space to erect the a table and host matches.

In 1969 the staff, now numbering a hundred, moved to Aykley Heads House. The distinguished 17th century building - complete with resident ghost, the Grey Lady - then shared the site with two wooden huts. Lawyers

Below: *Aykley Heads House.*

and administrators took the high-ceilinged house: legal and plans case workers took the huts.

Recruitment was steady as registration of property transactions became compulsory throughout most of Durham in the 1970s. New machines arrived. Typewriters became electric. Two photocopiers, each the size of a small car, loomed in one corner occasionally catching fire. The first computer terminals were installed.

By the end of the 1970s even Aykley Heads was too small. Southfield House, the Durham District Land registry's first purpose-built home, was opened in 1983. A planning stipulation for the structure, set low into the hillside between Dryburn Hospital and Whitesmocks, was that it had to be invisible from the cathedral.

In 1993 a decision was made to transfer responsibility for land registrations in Surrey up to Durham. As a result some staff moved to the newly-built Boldon House on the edge of the city next to the Arnison Centre.

Today Southfield House and Boldon House form part of a network of 24 local Land Registry offices running the world's largest database of its kind. The guarantee of title under the land registration system supports and simplifies millions of property transactions in England and Wales every year.

Where once the register was closed to public inspection and guarded in the finest traditions of the Civil Service, each

office now welcomes enquiries and can supply information immediately during office hours.

The typewriter, the paper maps and the messengers have now gone. Even the traditional plans/legal division amongst staff has disappeared, with caseworkers now creating both registers and plans at their computers.

Where once there was an ashtray on every desk both buildings now have gyms. Southfield House has a nursery for all Registry staff's children

But some things have not changed. There is a long tradition of community involvement: not only through charitable fund-raising for hospital and hospice but also through partnership with local schools.

Southfield House and Boldon House are proud to represent a government agency that upholds the highest public service values. An original winner of the Charter Mark in 1992, it is one of the few organisations to have held it continuously ever since. Strong community links are vital to that success. To quote the Chief Executive Peter Collis 'We have tried to be an organisation that keeps its feet on the ground, and our first objective is to meet the needs of today's customers making sure we provide the best possible service'.

Top left: *Southfield House.*
Below: *Boldon House.*

A place to call home

Today's Three Rivers Housing Group began life as the Three Rivers Housing Society in 1971. It became a Registered Social Landlord (and hence, became a Housing Association) in 1974 when the government formed the Housing Corporation. The Housing Corporation's remit was to fund the development of decent properties to rent, at affordable rates, for people in need.

A group of businessmen with an interest in providing co-ownership housing in what is the now the St Margaret Court site in Durham City founded the Three Rivers Housing Society. The founders included Professor Fisher, Steve Skene - a local solicitor and Tyrell Brockbank - Lord Lieutenant of County Durham and former Chief Executive of Durham County Council.

Throughout the whole period of Three Rivers' existence a Board of Management, which consists of people in the region in various occupations and positions voluntarily giving their time, has steered its direction.

As the government moved towards funding the development of properties to rent, the original aim to provide co-ownership homes also changed in line with the government's objectives. Yet today the Housing Group still offers home ownership schemes that resemble the original idea its founders had.

In the 1970s and 1980s there was the issue of who would take on the declining communities in former colliery villages. This led to significant investments in Dean Bank, Ferryhill Station and Sherburn Road estate in Durham, bringing better standard affordable housing to rent. Private financing to fund developments was introduced in 1989.

Another major challenge involved co-operation with the Teesside Development Corporation Marina in Hartlepool, being proactive in housing and communities under the Community Care Act 1991.

The very first scheme to be developed was Dunelm Court in Brandon, just on the outskirts of Durham. That scheme was made up of 62 units of flats and houses - these remain popular today. Since then the Housing Group has grown and now has more than 2,700 properties in the North East.

Those properties are spread from the south of the Tyne to Redcar and Cleveland. Durham however has the largest proportion of the properties.

In 1990 Three Rivers Housing Group opened its first home improvement agency under the name 'Care and Repair Derwentside'. This is a service which provides a renovation and adaptation service to homeowners and residents who are elderly, disabled or are otherwise vulnerable, enabling them to live independently in their homes. Today Three Rivers Housing Group operates four Care and Repair agencies in the

North East - East Durham, Darlington and the Redcar & Cleveland areas.

When the Three Rivers Housing Association was first set up in 1974 and based at 52 Old Elvet, there were only two members of staff - General Manager Gordon Kyle and a part-time secretary. By 1978 it had six full time and two part time staff. Gordon Kyle would be succeeded by Doug Hollingworth and later by Martin Nurse. Today's Chief Executive Martin Knowles heads a team of over 120 people working for Three Rivers Housing Group which is now based at Three Rivers House on the Abbeywoods Business Park after having relocated there via successively larger offices in Saddler Street and Hallgarth Street.

In the early days mainly rehabilitated older properties and small one-bedroom flats were made available. Now it is mainly newly-built properties and larger properties to meet today's expectations.

Today Three Rivers Housing Group has a diverse range of customers: both young and elderly single people, families, those working and those not in work, people who need extra care and support, people who are part-owners in a home ownership scheme, leaseholders as well as home-owners who benefit from the Care & Repair service that provides renovations and adaptations to enable people to remain in their own homes.

In the case of supported housing the Housing Group is increasingly helping people with disabilities to live more independently by offering new models of accommodation. For example, people with physical disabilities who may have lived in a care home now have the option of living in a self-contained flat with a communal area in a separate building.

For the future Three Rivers Housing Group aims to continue to grow, continuing its work in partnership with the public and private sector to meet the needs of communities and helping build better neighbourhoods for all.

Top left: *The Group's first scheme, Dunelm Court, Brandon.* ***Below:*** *Schooner Court, Hartlepool, one of Three Rivers' early developments.*

In the picture

The second half of the 20th century was almost defined by the appearance of the domestic television set. The TV is our window on the world. Television ownership received a major boost in 1953 as folk clamoured to see for themselves the coronation of Elizabeth II. Since then televisions have ceased to be a luxury affordable to only the lucky few and become familiar objects to be found in almost every home and office.

Now the 21st century is being defined by the computer screen. But, whilst almost everyone sees some kind of TV screen nearly every day, few are aware that one in four TV sets sold in Europe have a Durham cathode ray tube inside them.

Though technology is ever-evolving most televisions still rely on the modern day successor to the cathode ray tube invented as long ago as 1897 by Karl Ferdinand Braun. That invention led to the first black and white television tube in the late 1930s, and in due course to the modern wide-screen colour tube.

LG Philips Displays, based on the Belmont Industrial Estate, is the city's largest private employer with some 800 staff. An amazing three million tubes are now being made there every single year. There have been 50 million made so far.

Above: The Prime Minster Edward Heath chats to a member of staff at the opening of the factory in 1972.
Below: A general view of the Flowcoat Room where the three colour phosphors were laid on the tube's faceplate, 1977.

The factory was opened in 1972 by Prime Minster Edward Heath. The firm can however trace its origins back much further than 1972.

Stanley Mullard founded the Mullard Valve Company in the 1920s, though by the 1970s this had become a subsidiary of Philips.

Philips had in fact bought the Mullard Valve Company in the 1930s, but until the 1980s the Mullard name was retained. As a result the Durham plant would be known as Mullards by local folk until the 1980s when, for reasons of corporate identity, all Philips plants across the whole of Europe lost their historic names and all took the name of Philips.

The new Durham plant was designed to complement the activities of the Mullard tube-making and glass producing technology centre near Burnley in Lancashire. Glass parts from Lancashire would be finished and assembled in Durham.

Work began on the Durham site towards the end of 1970 and the £10 million factory was opened on 1st December 1971.

The new 420,000 sq ft plant occupied a 47 acre site three miles from the centre of Durham. The state of the art plant featured 10,000 feet of conveyors and a water intake capacity of 11,000 gallons an hour - the latter necessary since the manufacture of TV picture tubes involved a number of chemical processing steps each needing to be followed by a rinsing operation. Any fears of chemical pollution were allayed by a prize winning effluent treatment plant.

No expense was spared in order to leap frog both the technology and quality standards achieved by other manufacturers. Automated test consoles, each fully programmed to conduct the whole of the final testing would be installed at a cost of £42,000 each.

New employees were recruited locally from all backgrounds: mining, engineering and textiles. Many also came from rival firms such as Thorns in Sunderland.

Within a year some 800 employees were hard at work; strange as it now seems almost all were men, with only some 60 women employed on 'gun assembly'.

The workforce would eventually rise to a high of 1500. Manufacturing was a continuous process 24 hours a day over a five day period to turn out half a million 'Colourscreen' picture tubes each year.

Created in 2001, through the merger of the display businesses of Royal Philips Electronics of the Netherlands and LG Electronics of South Korea, today LG Philips Displays is the world's largest manufacturer of cathode ray tubes. The company with its headquarters in Hong Kong employs in total more than 24,000 people in 23 factories in 14 countries.

Over the last half century black and white tubes have been succeeded by colour, curved screens by flat. New picture display technology in the form of LCD and plasma screens is now appearing. Since 1971 Durham has been at the cutting edge of display technology and today staff at LG Philips are determined to ensure that the traditional cathode ray tube continues to keep the world in the picture.

Top left: *The Aluminising Department, 1970s.*
Below: *The L G Philips Displays factory, Belmont Industrial Estate.*

Moving the earth

Ever wondered where all those lorries, excavators and stone crushers come from that you see around large quarries and similar operations? Ward Bros Plant Hire Ltd based at Langley Moor operates one of the largest hire fleets in the country.

The company was founded in 1964 by Alan Ward, his family and brother Thomas. Until then Alan had been a third generation dairy farmer at Eastgate in Weardale.

Alan bought into an existing road haulage company owned by Percy Reed which had existing contracts hauling raw fluorspar from local mines to processing plants in Rookhope. From there the finished product was bagged for distribution - until in the late 1960s a fleet of bulk powder tankers was introduced of which three Gardner powered ERF wagons did in excess of one million miles each.

At first the business was run from the newly acquired company depot at Bolts Burn Garage, Rookhope and several years later transferred to the new premises at Frosterley, Weardale.

For the next 30 years or more haulage work mainly involved moving cement from Eastgate Cement Works, operated by Angus Ward.

Meanwhile the plant hire component of the business started in around 1965 at Rookhope; this expanded rapidly. Wards needed to be close to its market place and moved to Trimdon to be near collieries then owned by NCB. An NCB contract had been secured there in the late 1960s to supply all mobile surface plant in the area. From NCB collieries Ward Bros proceeded into civil engineering, open cast mining, and to today's key activities of contract crushing and skip hire.

Ian Ward was instrumental in seeing the opportunity in plant hire, his brothers Angus, Maxwell and Stewart eventually left farming behind them renting the farm off to others. All four were now involved in both plant hire and haulage.

Today, with the next Ward generation already involved, the company continues to be heavily involved in mobile crushing and general plant hire. The developing skip business is a key focus of future activity, whilst waste recycling is becoming a major part of business with Ward Bros now building a new facility to service Durham and surrounding area.

Top left: Founder, Alan Ward.
Below: The three Gardner powered ERF wagons which clocked up in excess of one million miles each, pictured with their drivers. *Inset:* Ward Bros fleet of skip wagons.

The age of plastic

We've had the stone age and the iron age. Modern times will surely be described by future historians as the Age of Plastic. Hillside Plastics Ltd was founded in 1971 by three work colleagues.

Peter Pounder, Alex Bell and Kevin Brooks had experience in plastic moulding and tool making. With the help of their bank manager and accountant they got themselves acquainted with activities such as book keeping, purchasing and estimating too.

The name Hillside was chosen because one of the original sites considered for setting up the business was on a hillside. Although the site was never used for injection moulding it was later acquired for ancillary assembly and storage.

A 2,000 sq ft unit was leased on the Meadowfield Industrial Estate, Brandon. With limited resources one moulding machine was purchased on a three year HP agreement, in the hope of generating enough income to progress.

By 1977 larger premises were needed. A purpose built unit of 10,000 sq ft was erected on the Meadowfield Estate.

Over the years the range of customers would be wide: Lucas Electrical, Aladdin Industries, Flymo and Wilkinson Sword. Black & Decker recognised Hillside's quality by awarding its Gold performance certificate, the first to be won by a UK moulding supplier .

Hillside Plastics set up a sister company in the Czech Republic to continue supplying Black & Decker since the transfer of its production in 2002.

Sadly co-founder Peter Pounder died in 1974 aged just 51.

Alex Bell died in 1990 aged 62; his son Tony followed him in the business and played a major part in the continuing expansion of the company. Tony has since left to explore pastures new. Kevin Brooks retired in 1994. Kevin's son Neil joined the company from leaving school; he and Michael Carrick, a former toolmaker, are the company's current Directors.

Hillside Plastics now runs 40 moulding machines over two sites. With an annual turnover of more than £5 million the Age of Plastic looks set fair to continue far into the foreseeable future.

Top: *Hillside Plastics Ltd's machinery of 1978.*
Left: *Joan Rutter and Kevin Brooks receive the Black & Decker Vendor of Excellence award on behalf of Hillside Plastics Ltd, 1990.*

Acknowledgments

The publishers would like to thank

Beamish Photograph Library at Beamish Museum

Julian Harrop

Andrew Mitchell

Steve Ainsworth

True North Books Ltd - Book List

Memories of Accrington - 1 903204 05 4

Memories of Barnet - 1 903204 16 X

Memories of Barnsley - 1 900463 11 3

More Memories of Barnsley - 1 903 204 79 8

Golden Years of Barnsley -1 900463 87 3

Memories of Basingstoke - 1 903204 26 7

Memories of Bedford - 1 900463 83 0

More Memories of Bedford - 1 903204 33 X

Golden Years of Birmingham - 1 900463 04 0

Birmingham Memories - 1 903204 45 3

More Birmingham Memories - 1 903204 80 1

Memories of Blackburn - 1 900463 40 7

More Memories of Blackburn - 1 900463 96 2

Memories of Blackpool - 1 900463 21 0

Memories of Bolton - 1 900463 45 8

More Memories of Bolton - 1 900463 13 X

Bolton Memories - 1 903204 37 2

Memories of Bournemouth -1 900463 44 X

Memories of Bradford - 1 900463 00 8

More Memories of Bradford - 1 900463 16 4

More Memories of Bradford II - 1 900463 63 6

Bradford Memories - 1 903204 47 X

Bradford City Memories - 1 900463 57 1

Memories of Bristol - 1 900463 78 4

More Memories of Bristol - 1 903204 43 7

Memories of Bromley - 1 903204 21 6

Memories of Burnley - 1 900463 95 4

Golden Years of Burnley - 1 900463 67 9

Memories of Bury - 1 900463 90 3

More Memories of Bury - 1 903 204 78 X

Memories of Cambridge - 1 900463 88 1

Memories of Cardiff - 1 900463 14 8

More Memories of Cardiff - 1 903204 73 9

Memories of Carlisle - 1 900463 38 5

Memories of Chelmsford - 1 903204 29 1

Memories of Cheltenham - 1 903204 17 8

Memories of Chester - 1 900463 46 6

More Memories of Chester -1 903204 02 X

Memories of Chesterfield -1 900463 61 X

More Memories of Chesterfield - 1 903204 28 3

Memories of Colchester - 1 900463 74 1

Nostalgic Coventry - 1 900463 58 X

Coventry Memories - 1 903204 38 0

Memories of Croydon - 1 900463 19 9

More Memories of Croydon - 1 903204 35 6

Golden Years of Darlington - 1 900463 72 5

Nostalgic Darlington - 1 900463 31 8

Darlington Memories - 1 903204 46 1

Memories of Derby - 1 900463 37 7

More Memories of Derby - 1 903204 20 8

Memories of Dewsbury & Batley - 1 900463 80 6

Memories of Doncaster - 1 900463 36 9

More Memories of Doncaster - 1 903204 75 5

Nostalgic Dudley - 1 900463 03 2

Golden Years of Dudley - 1 903204 60 7

Memories of Edinburgh - 1 900463 33 4

More memories of Edinburgh - 1903204 72 0

Memories of Enfield - 1 903204 14 3

Memories of Exeter - 1 900463 94 6

Memories of Glasgow - 1 900463 68 7

More Memories of Glasgow - 1 903204 44 5

Memories of Gloucester - 1 903204 04 6

Memories of Grimsby - 1 900463 97 0

More Memories of Grimsby - 1 903204 36 4

Memories of Guildford - 1 903204 22 4

Memories of Halifax - 1 900463 05 9

More Memories of Halifax - 1 900463 06 7

Golden Years of Halifax - 1 900463 62 8

Nostalgic Halifax - 1 903204 30 5

Memories of Harrogate - 1 903204 01 1

Memories of Hartlepool - 1 900463 42 3

Memories of High Wycombe - 1 900463 84 9

Memories of Huddersfield - 1 900463 15 6

More Memories of Huddersfield - 1 900463 26 1

Golden Years of Huddersfield - 1 900463 77 6

Nostalgic Huddersfield - 1 903204 19 4

Huddersfield Town FC - 1 900463 51 2

Memories of Hull - 1 900463 86 5

More Memories of Hull - 1 903204 06 2

Hull Memories - 1 903204 70 4

Memories of Ipswich - 1 900463 09 1

More Memories of Ipswich - 1 903204 52 6

True North Books Ltd - Book List

Memories of Kingston - 1 903204 24 0

Memories of Leeds - 1 900463 75 X

More Memories of Leeds - 1 900463 12 1

Golden Years of Leeds - 1 903204 07 0

Memories of Leicester - 1 900463 08 3

Leeds Memories - 1 903204 62 3

More Memories of Leicester - 1 903204 08 9

Memories of Leigh - 1 903204 27 5

Memories of Lincoln - 1 900463 43 1

Memories of Liverpool - 1 900463 07 5

More Memories of Liverpool - 1 903204 09 7

Liverpool Memories - 1 903204 53 4

Memories of Luton - 1 900463 93 8

Memories of Macclesfield - 1 900463 28 8

Memories of Manchester - 1 900463 27 X

More Memories of Manchester - 1 903204 03 8

Manchester Memories - 1 903204 54 2

Memories of Middlesbrough - 1 900463 56 3

More Memories of Middlesbrough - 1 903204 42 9

Memories of Newbury - 1 900463 79 2

Memories of Newcastle - 1 900463 81 4

More Memories of Newcastle - 1 903204 10 0

Newcastle Memories - 1.903204 71 2

Memories of Newport - 1 900463 59 8

Memories of Northampton - 1 900463 48 2

More Memories of Northampton - 1 903204 34 8

Memories of Norwich - 1 900463 73 3

Memories of Nottingham - 1 900463 91 1

More Memories of Nottingham - 1 903204 11 9

Nottingham Memories - 1 903204 63 1

Bygone Oldham - 1 900463 25 3

Memories of Oldham - 1 900463 76 8

Memories of Oxford - 1 900463 54 7

Memories of Peterborough - 1 900463 98 9

Golden Years of Poole - 1 900463 69 5

Memories of Portsmouth - 1 900463 39 3

More Memories of Portsmouth - 1 903204 51 8

Nostalgic Preston - 1 900463 50 4

More Memories of Preston - 1 900463 17 2

Preston Memories - 1 903204 41 0

Memories of Reading - 1 900463 49 0

Memories of Rochdale - 1 900463 60 1

More Memories of Reading - 1 903204 39 9

More Memories of Rochdale - 1 900463 22 9

Memories of Romford - 1 903204 40 2

Memories of Rothertham- 1903204 77 1

Memories of St Albans - 1 903204 23 2

Memories of St Helens - 1 900463 52 0

Memories of Sheffield - 1 900463 20 2

More Memories of Sheffield - 1 900463 32 6

Golden Years of Sheffield - 1 903204 13 5

Memories of Slough - 1 900 463 29 6

Golden Years of Solihull - 1 903204 55 0

Memories of Southampton - 1 900463 34 2

More Memories of Southampton - 1 903204 49 6

Memories of Stockport - 1 900463 55 5

More Memories of Stockport - 1 903204 18 6

Memories of Stockton - 1 900463 41 5

Memories of Stoke-on-Trent - 1 900463 47 4

More Memories of Stoke-on-Trent - 1 903204 12 7

Memories of Stourbridge - 1903204 31 3

Memories of Sunderland - 1 900463 71 7

More Memories of Sunderland - 1 903204 48 8

Memories of Swindon - 1 903204 00 3

Memories of Uxbridge - 1 900463 64 4

Memories of Wakefield - 1 900463 65 2

More Memories of Wakefield - 1 900463 89 X

Nostalgic Walsall - 1 900463 18 0

Golden Years of Walsall - 1 903204 56 9

More Memories of Warrington - 1 900463 02 4

Memories of Watford - 1 900463 24 5

Golden Years of West Bromwich - 1 900463 99 7

Memories of Wigan - 1 900463 85 7

Golden Years of Wigan - 1 900463 82 2

More Memories of Wigan - 1 903204 82 8

Nostalgic Wirral - 1 903204 15 1

Wirral Memories - 1 903204 747

Memories of Woking - 1 903204 32 1

Nostalgic Wolverhampton - 1 900463 53 9

Wolverhampton Memories - 1 903204 50 X

Memories of Worcester - 1 903204 25 9

Memories of Wrexham - 1 900463 23 7

Memories of York - 1 900463 66 0

Available in the Local Interest section of all major bookshops or direct from the publishers - telephone 01422 344344